ENGLISH
PAINTED ENAMELS

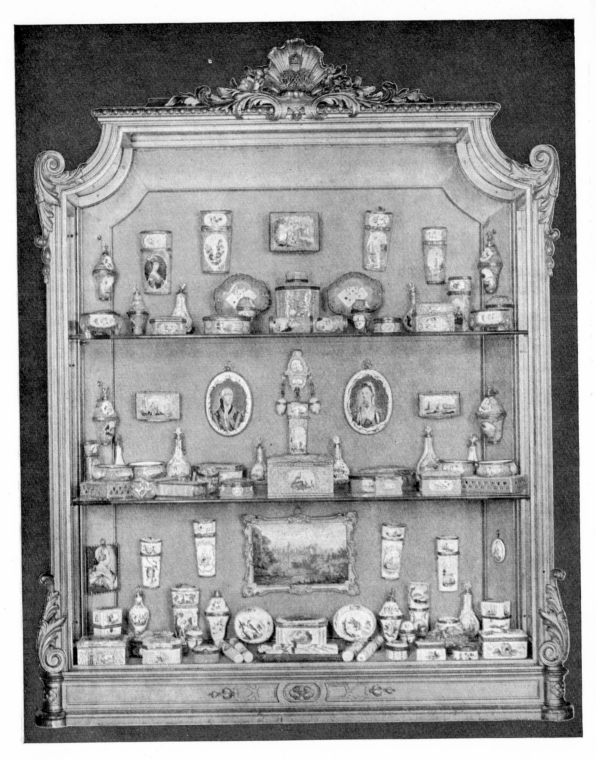

A vitrine containing a portion of the late Queen Mary's collection of English painted enamels.

ENGLISH PAINTED ENAMELS

THERLE & BERNARD HUGHES

SPRING BOOKS

Printed in Czechoslovakia by Tisk, Brno

CONTENTS

ILLUSTRATIONS

ACKNOWLEDGEMENTS

In the collection of the late Queen Mary:

Colour plates: Frontispiece, I, II, III

Black and white photographs: 1, 12, 13, 14, 23 (upper photograph), 24, 31, 32, 33, 35, 36, 37, 48, 57, 58, 63, 65, 68, 74, 79, 80, 81

In the Collection of the Hon. Mrs Ionides:

Black and white photographs: 2, 3, 4, 5, 6, 7, 8, 9, 10, 11, 15, 16, 17, 18, 19, 20, 21, 22, 23 (lower photograph), 25, 26, 27, 28, 29, 30, 34, 38, 39, 40, 41, 42, 43, 44, 45, 46, 47, 49, 50, 51, 52, 53, 54, 55, 56, 59, 60, 61, 62, 64, 66, 67, 69, 70, 71, 72, 73, 75, 76, 77, 78, 82

In the Victoria and Albert Museum: 83

IN COLOUR

IN BLACK AND WHITE

10

ENGLISH
PAINTED ENAMELS

PREFACE

ENGLISH painted and printed enamels were produced to meet a need for small personal luxuries that would prove sturdy and serviceable as well as essentially decorative. Basically they constituted an exciting and wholly English commercial venture, and their very success both at home and abroad is in itself some justification for this consideration of their story. But even at the time of their creation it was obvious to the discriminating that they were considerably more than a commercial success. As early as 1755 they had been 'discovered' by such connoisseurs as Horace Walpole, and the two succeeding centuries have left the collector's appreciation of their appeal as unsullied and undiminished as their own gay ornamentation. In the course of years, however, many details concerning their production have become obscure. Around the name of Battersea a wealth of legends has grown, making unnecessary mystery of Janssen's venture and distorting the whole picture of English enamels. The purpose of this book is to create at least an outline of this craft, in the light of present knowledge, which may more accurately establish its artistic accomplishment, its manufacturing techniques, and the individual contributions of some of the men responsible for its far from negligible achievements.

In preparing this work the authors have enjoyed opportunities of inspecting and examining many hundreds of enamels with a thoroughness made possible only by unbounded tolerance and generosity on the part of their owners. The late Queen Mary graciously allowed them the unique privilege of studying her collection of exceptionally fine specimens at Marlborough House: through the photographs of examples in these pages, others may now share this delight. With the same understanding and helpfulness the Hon. Mrs Ionides has given the authors constant access to her incomparable collection at Buxted and the incalculable benefit of her own experience in pursuit of these intriguing trifles. Without such assistance this book could never have been written. For some facts in connection with Bilston enamels thanks are due to Mr William H. Bowers of Stone.

Nevertheless, the authors regard it as no more than an introduction to a subject about which much has yet to be discovered or confirmed. Their hope is that it may stimulate others to pursue the matter further, to identify and discard valueless imitations, and bring the right emphasis of appreciation to the various phases in a notable contribution to England's industrial arts.

Chapter One

THE EARLY ENAMELLERS

ENAMELLING is one of the oldest of decorative crafts and one of the most permanent. Specimens over a thousand years old retain something of their beauty to this day—mere fragments of coloured glass, yet rich and radiant as jewels. Indeed the work of the enameller has always been closely allied with that of the goldsmith, whose precious metals have served as perfect foils for the enamels' splendid colours.

Given the widest meaning, the term enamel covers a range of vitreous substances, some semi-transparent, some completely opaque, used for covering or ornamenting, by the process of fusion, the surfaces of metals, porcelain, and glass. To the collector, however, the process most generally termed enamelling consists of fusing a paste of powdered glass on to a base of metal, usually gold, copper, or bronze. The moistened enamel powder is spread thinly over the metal object which is then fired in the kiln, the heat melting the enamel so that it adheres in a smoothly lustrous coating. Various colours, clear or opaque, are achieved by the admixture of metallic oxides, but the craft had been practised for many centuries before much attempt was made to create brush-painted pictorial effects.

In this book it is proposed to deal in detail with the form of enamelling that won particular renown for the artist-craftsmen of eighteenth-century England. In the light of widespread recent research this must include not only the brief radiance that was Battersea but the more enduring manufactories of Birmingham and South Staffordshire whose managers called upon the native skill of the country's finest metal-workers and the decorative genius of many unknown artists and engravers.

In order to see this wholly charming contribution to our country's industrial art in its right perspective, however, it is necessary to appreciate what had, and what had not, been achieved by earlier enamellers throughout the long and colourful story of their craft.

During its development there have been three main methods of applying decorative enamels to metal:

1. *Cloisonné and Champlevé.* In *cloisonné* enamel the colour divisions making up the pattern are outlined on a metal ground by raised metal partitions. In the *champlevé* method, the same effect is achieved by tiny walls in the solid metal of the background, between which hollows are scooped out to hold the vari-coloured enamels.

2. *Basse-taille.* In this form of enamelling the metal surface itself is first worked in low relief. When it is covered with translucent enamels the design is depicted by the varying depths of enamel and consequent variation in the intensity of the colours.

3. *Painted Enamels.* Here the enamel covering the metal base is brush-decorated with enamels in contrasting colours and serves as does a canvas in oil painting or the ivory of a miniature.

The early history of enamelling is obscure and the origin of many existing specimens is open to speculation. The immense renown of the illuminator and embroiderer in early Christian Britain, however, and the Celtic character of surviving pieces, support the claim of those who believe that this country played a notable part in the development of this kindred craft. The oldest known enamels on metal have been ascribed to Greek and Etruscan origin, between the sixth and third centuries B.C. At least as early as the later date Celtic craftsmen were applying enamels to cast bronzes, and during the Roman occupation a greater range of colours appeared in enamelled brooches, harness pieces, and so on, made in Britain as in other Roman provinces.

These early enamellers formed shallow designs in the surface of their metal, usually bronze, and filled the depressions with coloured enamels. By restricting the enamels to small areas they minimized subsequent flaking and, equally important, kept the different colours from flowing into each other when melted in the firing process. In the final result the partitions showed

1. Battersea plaque, $4\frac{1}{2} \times 3\frac{1}{2}$ inches, of Prince George, eldest son of Frederick, Prince of Wales. Transfer–printed in brown, this is identical with prints issued by William Sandby, appropriately captioned, both before and after the future King George III was created Prince of Wales in 1751. In taking this study from the painting by Richard Wilson, Ravenet reversed the figure and added the Garter star and ribbon.

2. Four medallions, all $3\frac{3}{8} \times 2\frac{3}{4}$ inches, decorated with monochrome transfer-prints accredited to Battersea. *Top:* Two subjects taken from Ravenet engravings, William Augustus, Duke of Cumberland, and his father George II. The latter is a reproduction of John Sigismund Tanner's engraving made for the country's coinage. *Below, left:* Robert Walpole, first Earl of Orford, taken from the portrait by J. B. van Loo painted in 1740 and now in the National Gallery. Face and hair—reversed from the original—appear to be Ravenet's work although the dress details may have been added by another hand. *Right:* Maria Gunning, Countess of Coventry. The source of the engraving from which this was made is a painting by Francis Cotes dated 1751, but the engraver is unknown and the print lacks some of the Ravenet characteristics.

18

3. A cabinet of English painted enamels from the Ionides collection. The central plaque above the second shelf was long thought to be of Janssen but has now been identified by the Hon. Mrs Ionides as being 'The Right Honble. William Beckford Esqr'.

4. 'Venus and Triton', a plaque transfer-printed in a lilac shade showing the graceful flowing movement associated with Ravenet's Battersea work.

5. A notably large plaque $6\frac{3}{4} \times 4\frac{1}{2}$ inches, palely transfer-printed in indigo. The style of engraving and details of face and draperies are reminiscent of Ravenet, and the fact that the enamel has cracked badly and has not been framed may suggest that this was an experimental piece of Battersea work.

20

6. Two boxes, measuring approximately $3\frac{1}{4} \times 2\frac{3}{4} \times 1\frac{1}{4}$ inches, the lids decorated with monochrome transfer-prints from engravings by Ravenet and assumed to be Battersea products. *Left:* The Trojan priest Laocoön with the Grecian wooden horse. Inside the lid is a print of Robert Walpole similar to that in Plate 2, and on the sides are Ravenet transfer-prints of *putti*. *Right:* Britannia presenting coins to Science and the Arts. Inside the lid is another Ravenet transfer-print of George II (illustrated in Plate 2), taken from the contemporary coinage design. A noteworthy feature is the scroll-surrounded diaper pattern on the rest of the box, flatly transfer-printed. This was the forerunner of the raised decoration of South Staffordshire (see page 61).

7. *Left:* Paris awarding the apple to Hibernia under the approving eye of Britannia—a Ravenet transfer-subject probably from an original by James Gwim. *Above:* A later rendering in the South Staffordshire style. The picture is reversed by the inexpert engraver, making the characters left-handed, and the heavy transfer-print is touched with colours.

21

8. Plaque of a Judgement scene taken from the engravings of Christ's Passion by Sébastien le Clerc the elder (d. 1714): 'Christ before Caiaphas'.

9. St James of Compostella, a plaque 3½ × 2½ inches at its greatest diameter. The transfer-print, ascribed to Ravenet, has been washed with colours—brown robes and green ground, and a golden halo.

10. 'The Return from the Garden of Gethsemane'—a companion plaque to that in Plate 8. The bright, cold colours are those associated with early Battersea work—deep pink, vivid blue and pale yellow over outlines in red.

22

11. Two enamel snuff-boxes transfer-printed in near-black. Modifications of these designs constantly appear on painted enamels, taken from the pattern book of about 1760 entitled *The Ladies Amusement*. On the left is a fine rendering of Watteau's *Fêtes Champêtres*, engraved by Laurent Cars (1699–1771) under the title *Fêtes Vénitiennes*. This is reversed from the original painting and the musicians play a fiddle and flute instead of bagpipes. *The Ladies Amusement* reproduced only the dancing lady and the two musicians in an anonymous engraving. The long-tailed parrot among the fruit suggests the work of Robert Hancock, who engraved a rather similar but better poised design for *The Ladies Amusement*—possibly a later version.

12. Two boxes with some stylistic resemblances. The yellow snuff-box (*left*), $3\frac{1}{2} \times 2\frac{5}{8} \times 1\frac{3}{8}$ inches, has its lid entirely covered with a rendering of 'The Corner Game'. The original, *Le Jeu de Quatre-Coins* by Nicolas Lancret, was engraved by Nicolas de Larmessin in 1737 and this was copied by Robert Hancock (see page 59). On this box the liquid, bright colours appear to have been applied over a transfer-print. Flowers in full colours decorate the sides and there is a single flower on the base. The tobacco-box, $4\frac{3}{4} \times 2\frac{3}{8} \times 1\frac{5}{8}$ inches, has its concave sides and its base somewhat similarly painted with flowers. The subject on the lid is taken from the painting by Watteau, *Le Colin-Maillard*, from another design by Claude Gillot, *Les Vendages* or *Le Toucher*. Watteau's painting was engraved by E. Brion.

13. *Above:* Two views of a double box with an interior partition and both top and base forming hinged lids decorated with full colour paintings. The shaped sides carry flower posies on a hard white ground. The principal view is of Orleans House, Twickenham, now the property of the Hon. Mrs Ionides and appearing on several articles in her collection. It is taken from an engraving entitled 'Governor Pitt's House (late Secretary Johnson's) at Twickenham' after a drawing by A. Heckell published 1749.

14. *Left:* Two views of a circular box, 2 inches in diameter, lavishly and individualistically painted in the early style on a ground of soft white enamel. The pictures on the sides are of harbour scenes.

as metal outlines, flush with the enamel surface after firing, grinding, and polishing. Colours included white, black, yellow, coral red, cobalt blue, and dark green. Delicate enamels made by this method have been found in this country decorating bronze bowls. They are considered to be of about the sixth or seventh century, and to be Celtic rather than Nordic in inspiration.

In this early work the bronze base clouded the enamels, the tin in the alloy making the colours wholly opaque. Only when goldsmiths developed the craft of *cloisonné* enamelling on a base of gold was there any suggestion of jewel-like translucency.

Cloisonné enamelling represents the jeweller's approach to enamel decoration. It is particularly associated with Byzantine work and suggests Persian influence, although it was practised in Ireland from very early times. The book of the monk Theophilus, written in the tenth or eleventh century when the craft was at its height, described minutely the method still used centuries later. The design was outlined on the gold ground by vertical metal strips or ribbons, only a fraction of an inch high, edge-soldered to the plate to form a series of tiny compartments which were filled with enamels. Jewellers had long been accustomed to mounting their stones in this manner. In some later *cloisonné* work, associated particularly with Russia and Hungary, wire was used to separate and support the enamels, often twisted like silken cord and suggestive of filigree work.

The rare variety of enamel known as *plique-à-jour* was a modification of the *cloisonné* particularly associated with Russia and Scandinavia. In this, semi-transparent, coloured enamel was vitrified in open-ended *cloisons* not attached to a metal base. These *cloisons* might be shaped from ribbons of gold or silver, or fret-cut from a sheet of the metal. The result when held to the light resembled a miniature stained-glass window. The earliest examples of this work date from about the eleventh century.

The interesting late-ninth-century Alfred jewel in the Ashmolean Museum, Oxford, is a *cloisonné* enamel, the craftsmanship of the metal-work distinguishing it from known contemporary Continental work. In the centre is a man, his head and arms in opaque enamel in contrast to the translucent blues and greens of which the remainder of the enamel is largely composed. In each hand he holds a sceptre or wand bursting into leaf, as so often appears in Celtic art, and he is surrounded by an inscription in Old English, 'Alfred me has worked'. In the British Museum is the brooch found on Dowgate Hill, attributed to the tenth century but less certainly of British origin, and it is largely by Continental references to Anglo-Saxon work that the scope of the craft in these obscure days can now be assessed.

The art of *cloisonné* enamelling was established in the Cologne district of Germany by the end of the tenth century. It was introduced by eastern craftsmen under the Byzantine princess Theophano when she married Otho II, Emperor of Germany, in 973. In early German work the gold background, variously decorated with engraving, set off the richly enamelled figure subject, but even by the twelfth century German enamellers were beginning to substitute cheaper copper or bronze for the gold used by their eastern masters and were applying the enamel more thickly. They then returned, as an obvious consequence, to the early method of hollowing out small compartments in the metallic ground itself to hold the colours separate during the firing process. This then became known as *champlevé* enamelling.

In adopting this process, the Germans were merely following the dictates of the material in which they worked. The desire to make larger decorative pieces first suggested the use of cheaper bronze or copper for the base, and this in turn suggested the adoption of the coppersmith's normal mode of work. For centuries the coppersmith had been accustomed to hollow out his metal as a basis for decoration in other metals—a method far easier than soldering on clumsy *cloisons* when the base metal could be comparatively thick without extravagance. Nevertheless, in Chinese work, now thought to have been introduced no earlier than the thirteenth century, the method was almost invariably *cloisonné* and yet the metal for the base was usually bronze. Some transitional German pieces show gold *cloisons* soldered to a copper base.

The presence of tin in the bronze base imposed its own restrictions on workers in *champlevé* enamel: it proved impossible to retain the translucence of the enamel, and this early *champlevé* work, like the earliest English enamels, was mainly opaque. As in the closely allied *cloisonné* work, the tiny compartments were filled with layers of enamel of the desired colours, leaving fine lines of metal level with the enamel surface. Gilding emphasized the exposed bronze, but the whole tendency now was towards a heraldic style of flat colour patchwork, as opposed to the intricate patterns of curving metal lines suited to the flexible ribbons of gold. Again it was the change in material that determined the course of the change in design. At the same time it became customary to leave much of the bronze uncovered, the rather clumsy work which could then be achieved with fired enamels being agreeably contrasted with gilded metal, which was engraved or chased. Figure work was easily produced when the face was of engraved metal and the enamel largely reserved for background effects.

By the twelfth century the craft of *champlevé* enamelling was becoming widespread, especially for ecclesiastical use, and enamellers were making more ambitious attempts to produce harmonies of tone. The Germans in particular now tended to let their colours blend and fuse into each other. Sometimes blurred dots and diaper effects were produced by making depressions in an area of enamel and filling them with another colour. The colours used were still limited to those obtained from various metallic oxides: copper produced red, green, and, with a soda base, turquoise blue; manganese produced various tones of purple; iron, a coral red, blue-green, and yellow-brown; cobalt, various shades of blue; tin, an opaque white; gold produced another tone of red, and silver produced yellow. To mix these colours in any way was expert work indeed.

Champlevé enamel decorated a wide variety of articles used for church ceremonial and personal ornament. These included crosses, reliquaries, triptyches and the like, sword hilts, belts, caskets, candlesticks, cups, basins, knife handles, rings, buttons, and brooches. The craft spread quickly from Cologne to the towns on the Meuse as far as Verdun. At this period there was considerable intercourse between English and Continental monasteries and it seems highly probable that various English establishments produced enamels with the same expertness and elaboration of detail that is seen in this country's contemporaneous illuminated manuscripts. Professor Tancred Borenius has drawn attention to the fact that the enamelled Warwick ciborium of about the twelfth century in the Victoria and Albert Museum shows several colours delicately fused together without metal partitions, and intricacies of floral work not seen in Continental products at this period. Similarly, by comparison with manuscripts and paintings of the time, the well-known Masters plaque at the same museum must be ascribed to the Winchester school of the twelfth century.

All too soon, however, the craft became peculiarly associated with the town of Limoges in central France, and there is evidence that even in England work was commissioned from this centre. Two thirteenth-century bishops of Winchester specifically commanded that the Host should be preserved in a ciborium of silver, ivory, or *opere Limovitico*. There are records, too, of Limoges workmen employed in England, such as Johannes Limovicensis who was commissioned in 1267 to erect an effigy of the Bishop of Rochester. English enamellers still undertook heraldic work, however, such as the stall plates of the Knights of the Garter in St George's Chapel, Windsor, dating from between 1370 and 1500. That the English thought highly of the craft is witnessed by the many contemporary references to presents made by royalty to the Pope and various foreign dignitaries. The Issue Roll of Edward III, for example, shows that in 1365 he bought from Thomas Hessey, a London goldsmith, fifty cups, ewers, and salts all silver-gilt and enamelled. There are contemporary records, too, of English goldsmith-enamellers working in Paris.

In Limoges itself, beginning in the monasteries early in the twelfth century, the craft soon developed in the district as a lay project, only to deteriorate into a vast commercial undertaking and then to disappear early in the fourteenth century. In some Limoges specimens a gilt background, variously ornamented with engraving, sets off the richly enamelled figure subject. But soon the craftsmen found it simpler to set gilded engraved metal figures against backgrounds of variously decorated enamels. Lapis blue was much used as a ground colour, with yellow and green, red, light blue, and white for ornament. At first the hands, then the whole figure, were often cast separately in relief and riveted to the piece, which gave every indication of commercialism. By then, however, Limoges enamels had a European reputation, their uses ranging from reliquary shrines and a wealth of other religious pieces to plaques for mounting on toilet- and jewel-boxes. The grave-plate of Geoffrey Plantagenet, in the museum of Le Mans, is the earliest known piece of Limoges *champlevé* and also the largest, measuring two feet by one foot. Some enamels of this period resembling *champlevé* were, in fact, based on *repoussé* work: the metal background was hammered up instead of being 'grounded out' to form the relief work between the colours.

While Limoges dominated the European market with commercially successful *champlevé* enamels, experiments in the craft continued elsewhere. Even before the end of the thirteenth century the Italians were beginning to develop new potentialities in the translucence which could be achieved with enamels fused upon a base of gold or silver and which are immensely enhanced by the light-catching irregularities of surface caused by the metal-worker's tooling. Developed by such craftsmen as John of Pisa (1250-1328), this work became known as *basse-taille* enamelling. It was particularly associated with silver plate for both church and laity, being produced also in France, especially in Paris, and in England. The metal ground, whether engraved, punched, or worked in *repoussé*, was designed in low relief so that, when filled with enamels, the varying depths and consequent colour intensities created the pattern.

The Florentine Benvenuto Cellini (1500-1571) described this process in detail in his *Treatise on Metal Work*. He stressed that, with careful firing, any number of different colours might be applied side by side in thin layers, always provided that preliminary tests showed that these 'ran' at the same temperature. In the Bodleian Library is a thirteenth-century psalter, its silver binding chased with the Annunciation and Coronation of the Virgin, covered with translucent enamel. This has been given a possible, but doubtful, English origin. Research suggests that English *basse-taille* craftsmen usually left the faces of their figures silver, whereas Continental enamellers covered them with enamel. Further examples of *basse-taille* work are seen on fourteenth- and fifteenth-century mitres and croziers, with brilliant translucent enamels on silver gilt. The fourteenth-century crozier of William of Wykeham has been classed by Professor Borenius as the finest surviving piece of medieval ecclesiastical enamel-work and undoubtedly of English workmanship.

The quintessence of purely decorative enamel was achieved at this period by those enamellers who backed their *champlevé* enamels with *paillons* of metal foil. Warm shades were backed with *paillons* of gold, and cool blues and greens with silver. These had the additional advantage of protecting the colours from becoming opacified or otherwise spoiled by the bronze base metal. Still associating the craft with that of the metal-worker rather than the painter, and softening the rather garish effects of the *paillons*, the enameller added delicate hatching lines of gold paint to pick out the high-lights on hair and draperies, or to pattern the background with stars. In reverse of this, some enamels were covered with gold-leaf and the designs traced with a fine needle-point, which removed the gold to reveal delicate lines of the under-lying coloured enamel.

Yet another technique, probably dating from the sixteenth century and associated with Venice, was indicative of formalistic Persian influence. Line arabesques were delicately painted in gold upon large areas of rich translucent colour and sealed by an outer coating of colourless enamel.

None of these ways of applying enamel, however, associated it in any great measure with pictorial art; it remained the metal-worker's province. Only at the end of the fifteenth century did enamellers begin to solve the technical problems involved in producing brush-painted pictures. First, the smooth undercoat of white enamel had to be made to adhere to a thin metal base without the aid of *cloisons*. Somewhat convex surfaces proved most successful.

These were enamelled on both sides so as to avoid warping. For the subsequent painting, exact regulation of furnace heat was required, coupled with skill in mixing various colours and fluxes so that the temperature at which each would melt was known. Coloured enamels could then be painted over each other and fixed by firings in the furnaces, each layer being mixed with softer fluxes requiring less heat to melt them, so that later firings would have no effect upon colours already fixed.

Some early painting in enamels was done in Italy, and some medallions in the British Museum have been ascribed to the school of Leonardo da Vinci in late fifteenth-century Milan. But it was in Limoges that this second great phase in enamel-work was developed, until these craftsmen could brush-paint in enamel upon enamelled metal just as the city's glass-workers had learnt to paint in enamels upon window glass.

It must be appreciated that the fixing of each colour by firing gave the artist's work a permanence incomparably greater than could be expected of the tempera and oil painting of the period, so that a tendency to aim at pictorial effects, away from the true decorative province of the enameller, was understandable. In some early painted enamels the place of the metal partitions between the colours was taken by heavy, very dark lines of enamel which outlined the design on the basic layer of enamel. These served to some extent to separate different colours fused by the one firing. The dark lines seen through translucent enamels gave outline and even some effect of three-dimensional shading to the decoration. Some opaque colours were also used.

Improvements in painted enamel occurred at least as early as the sixteenth century, but the enameller still found any semblance of flesh colour hard to achieve. Harsh opaque white was supplanted by an equally unsatisfactory pinkish-grey or lilac, consisting of white over a basis of manganese purple. This was used by Nardon Pénicaud and his followers, whose work was characterized by rich crimsons and blues and much delicate hatching in gold. The tints in these enamels were—and remain—extremely vivid, the whole conception of the work still being suggestive of the miniatures found in illuminated parchments of the period. If today they seem slightly garish, it must be remembered that they were largely intended for the dim light of church or home interiors.

Nardon Pénicaud, born 1474, the first of several enamellers of this name, was among the earliest notable Limoges painters in enamel. The first dated painted enamel is his representation of the Crucifixion executed in 1503. In the same tradition of vivid colour was the masterly portraitist in oils as well as enamels, Léonard Limousin (*d.* 1577), enameller to Francis I, whose signature or initials frequently appeared with a fleur-de-lis signifying his court appointment. His enamels still in existence include eleven of Francis I and ten of Henry II. He was well aware of the brilliant effects which could be achieved with *paillons* of metal foil, but it was left to lesser artists to practise this to excess, as seen in some late products from the prolific Courteys family.

As might be expected, the subjects of most early enamels had been religious and the art closely allied in feeling with contemporary stained-glass windows. The greater range of tone and delicacy of brush-work detail in painted work, combined with durability, at once recommended the craft for portraiture, but many other ambitious pictorial subjects were copied. When Albrecht Dürer began issuing wood and copper engravings around the turn of the sixteenth century these were seized upon by enamellers. Such scenes as Christ's Passion in rich Renaissance settings were entirely in keeping with the spirit of the enameller's craft. Other favourite subjects included St George and the dragon, Samson and the lion, and the story of Psyche. By the time enamelling in *grisaille* became established as the last great enamelling 'trade' of Limoges, French art had lost its medieval formalism and was largely under the spell of the art of the Italian Renaissance. Such vivid scenes as Raphael's fresco of the feast of the Gods on the marriage of Cupid and Psyche was evidently particularly popular.

This sixteenth-century *grisaille* enamel-work entirely lacked the splendour of rich, translucent colour that had been the enameller's greatest glory. The two styles of enamelling, in intensely vivid colour and in a narrow range of grey tones, were never wholly distinct. Some craftsmen, such as Léonard Limousin and Pierre Reymond, used both techniques; others approximated between the two with what is generally called tinted *grisaille*.

The *grisaille* was produced by a somewhat different technique from any formerly used and was a direct imitation of the onyx cameo of classical Rome. The copper plate was spread with a fairly heavy coat of intensely black enamel. (Less strictly the term *grisaille* may also be given to the large amount of work on coloured grounds, such as dark blue and dark brown.) This was vitrified in the oven, forming a uniform background which was covered with a filmy layer of finest quality white enamel, through which the dark colour glowed dimly. This opaque tin-white enamel had a volatile oil

31

base. It could be applied with a brush instead of the spatula required for the older style of enamelling, but it tended to be a rather heavy, blobby medium, and in order to achieve perfection of detail some artists chose to apply it thinly over the entire surface and then scrape it away with a needle-point from those areas and lines that were to appear dark in the final picture. After the scraping, the enamel was fixed by firing. Further layers of very thin white were similarly applied and partially scraped away, each layer more thoroughly obscuring the black base. By this method the enameller achieved an effect of delicate, slightly rounded modelling in a range of tones from deep grey to pure white, sufficient to give his picture definition and body. Finishing touches were put in with hatching lines in black and a little gold.

Undoubtedly many artists modified and simplified this work, treating it more straightforwardly as brush-painting, so far as their heavy medium would allow, but all aimed at a more or less three-dimensional picture entirely in white and greyish tones upon a deeper grey background. Some notable workers in *grisaille*, including Pierre Reymond, intensified the shadows by painting in many lines of hatching. They thus lost the harmony of the range of grey tones in an attempt to achieve the hard outlines of the contemporary engravings that they copied. Others again tinted their *grisaille* pictures with translucent colour.

Limoges *grisaille* enamels constituted pictorial art, but largely lacked the liquid colour that had caught the imagination of early enamellers. Later enamellers achieved greater freedom for pictorial or decorative expression, a wider range of colours and greater exactitude of brush-work, still enhanced by the assurance of durability given by repeated firings. But they never recaptured the old jewel-like fire. The vogue for miniature portraits painted in enamels lasted for more than two centuries. The drier, more prosaic, enamel colours came to be regarded merely as paints to produce opaque effects on white grounds which could be fired to ensure permanence. Their own inherent decorative value was lost.

Enamelling was distinctly a craft developed for its commercial possibilities. Its early application to metal-work used in churches and collected by the devout was long maintained, for it was an obvious vehicle for religious teaching, as colourful, if as primitive, as the sister art of the stained-glass window. The range of these enamels includes diptyches and triptyches, reliquaries, plaques and medallions, shrines, ciboria, croziers, and so on. But the trade in purely secular enamels was very considerable, and remaining specimens indicate the wide appreciation of enamel as a substitute for jewels on every kind of metal object. Innumerable plates, ewers, basins, salts, vases, and so on were produced. An enamelled girdle was specified as *façon d'Angleterre* in the possession of the Duke of Normandy in 1363. Stirrups, knife handles, exquisite gold cases for miniatures, and many species of jewellery were produced during the fifteenth and sixteenth centuries. But it was in the mid-eighteenth century that another chapter was added to the story of English enamel-work. At this time it was only to be expected that this would relate to painted enamel and that the work would display the fine taste and careful craftsmanship of its period. Today, indeed, these painted plaques, boxes, étuis, and other small *galanteries* seem to express the very spirit of the mid-eighteenth-century English scene.

As early as the fifteenth or sixteenth century medallions of Limoges enamel were applied as lids to little gilt-metal boxes, but the wide development of painted enamel snuff-boxes, cheaper but no less colourful than the jewelled gold creations they mimicked, largely dates from about 1750. By then it was being found that painted enamels could be applied as a commercial proposition to many little objects of personal luxury, giving them a decorative charm previously reserved mainly for the exclusive few who could afford the precious creations of the jeweller. These included snuff-boxes, étuis, watch-cases, and bonbonnières, all delicately decorated in full colours with copies of oil paintings, flowers and fruits, birds and animals. Jean Petitot (1608-1691), remembered as one of the finest miniaturist enamellers and represented by no fewer than two hundred and fifty examples of his work at Windsor Castle, began by decorating boxes and the like.

When the fashion for these bibelots reached England it caught the imagination of colour-loving early Georgian craftsmen. To such a state of artistic charm did they bring their work that English enamels found a ready market abroad as well as in this country, wherever ladies and gentlemen of fashion sought to buy exquisite trifles as gifts or souvenirs. And so considerable was their technical achievement that, after nearly two hundred years, colour and ornament are as clear and fresh today as when they were created, as small but distinctive expressions of discerning eighteenth-century taste.

Chapter Two

EXPERIMENTAL WORK
OF THE MID-XVIII CENTURY

THE early Byzantine jeweller used glass fused on to gold and silver in place of precious stones. The Georgian enameller used hand-painted and transfer-printed enamels fused on copper to make comparatively inexpensive trinkets imitating the costly bijouterie of Continental goldsmiths. To understand the real worth of the contribution made by English enamels to the minor crafts of the eighteenth century, it is essential to appreciate that while they were essentially decorative they were also unquestionably utilitarian. Once again the craft of the enameller was developed as a commercial proposition just as in earlier centuries it had met a vast demand for inexpensive yet vivid and enduring religious pieces. For the same reason, it was to be expected that the work would be imitative rather than creative. Even in China, Canton enamels were but cheaper copies of fragile porcelain. It is for this very reason all the more remarkable that English enamels of the eighteenth century possess a very real and endearing charm and individuality within the limits strictly imposed upon their creators.

Long before Stephen Theodore Janssen was persuaded to launch the Battersea enamelling venture in 1753 (see Chapter Three), the vogue for such bijouterie had been firmly established. Georgian England was renowned for the cultivation of the exterior graces and ornamental manners. In eager imitation of Continental extravagance, every detail of dress and behaviour became as studied—and as charming—as the steps in a minuet. The very snuff-box handed in greeting to an acquaintance in the Mall, the tiny flask of perfume designed to overcome the stifling atmosphere of the playhouse, had now to be in itself an exquisite trifle.

While these demands on taste and manners were confined to the rich and exclusive few, snuff-box and scent bottle were still the province of the jeweller. When the beau of 1730 contemplated presenting his lady with an enamelled box for sweetmeats or comfits, a tiny tablet for her engagements, or a *carnet de bal*, he thought in terms of the enamelled gold of France, or perhaps of Dresden or Geneva. These enamels were delicately painted with tiny pastoral scenes, with impish cupids and Boucher's lovely ladies, with simple little nosegays, or with fine portraits set in jewels. At a period when the tiniest gift must be in harmony with the mannered ritual of its presentation, it pleased the English gallant to see his little bibelot inscribed as a *Souvenir de l'amitié* or *Marque de mon estime*.

Such trifles were still essentially exclusive, however. The charm of these Continental luxuries depended upon their exquisite daintiness, and this necessitated the application of the enamel direct to a base of thinnest gold. When the base was made of copper of equal delicacy the enamel quickly fell away, and thicker copper produced weighty 'toys' unlikely to appeal to the fastidious dilettante. It was when a larger, slightly less wealthy, class of gallants sought the means to emulate the modish few, when London and the fashionable watering-places were thronged with men and women eager to reproduce these studied graces on a less lavish scale, that English craftsmen turned their inherent skill as artists, as craftsmen, and, above all, as improvisators, to the production, for instance, of Chelsea porcelain in imitation of Sèvres, of Bow *blanc de Chine*, of 'portraits' in wax, of innumerable imitation tortoiseshells, of printed fans—or of English painted enamels.

The whole of such meagre evidence as has yet been verified regarding the productions of the famous Battersea enamel factory indicates that when Janssen started in 1753 the project had every prospect of success. There was, already well established, the vogue for the type of elegant plaques 'for the cabinets of the curious', and a general demand and use for all the little boxes, watch-cases, toothpick-cases, wine-labels, buttons, and 'other curiosities' mentioned when this York House factory was sold up. There was a general acceptance of their style of decoration. The same flowers, birds, insects, and pastoral scenes, presented in profusion in such pattern books as Pillement's *Ladies Amusement*, appeared around the mid-eighteenth century on porcelain and needlework, on Liverpool tiles and Bristol glass. Moreover, recent research has brought to light the fact that there was already available the necessary technical knowledge filtering into this country from the Continent.

It was the peculiar achievement of Battersea that, while accepting the current terms and conditions of the English enamel trade, Janssen yet managed, in that brief and financially unsuccessful venture, to revolutionize the whole trend of English enamelling. In what was the first successful attempt to apply the mechanics of transfer-printing to the peculiar needs of opaque white enamel, and thus to prepare the way for all subsequent transfer-printing upon porcelain, he established standards of decorative quality, originality, and naïve gaiety which continued long after the Battersea factory itself was entirely forgotten.

Just how thoroughly the process of producing enamelled 'toys' in England had become established before Battersea opened is a subject requiring more attention than it has previously received.

The English enameller's problem in the 1740's—a problem ever recurrent in the long history of the craft—was to transfer the jeweller's creation, a costly individual work based on gold, into a cheaper yet acceptably dainty bibelot, factory-made on a basis of copper or bronze.

Some writers have suggested that the technical difficulties involved in securing the permanent adhesion of enamel to a paper-thin core of copper were overcome as the result of a discovery by some unidentified Englishman. The practical requirements of such an enamelling process are considered in detail in Chapter Six. But here attention must be drawn to the fact that in 1758 Robert Dossie, in his *Handmaid to the Arts*, referred to the enamellers of Geneva as already long experienced 'in this branch of commerce which gave them originally the greatest advantages in it over us'.

Exactly when the process was developed is, as yet, unknown. But that painted enamelling was established as a commercial process in London, probably a decade before Janssen's factory at Battersea opened its doors, is proved by *A General Description of all Trades*, published in 1747. This records that:

> Enamelling is a curious art, and not much labour but that of laying and painting colours, plain or in figures, on metal. The masters in this way are not many; but they will take with an apprentice £10, yet if the lad has not some genius as well as instruction he will not do well at it, as is indeed the case in several other arts. Their hours of business are from six in the morning to eight at night; in which time a good hand will

get three shillings or four shillings, and a person may set up for himself with a little money.

The painted enamels made by these pre-Battersea enamellers may be presumed to have resembled the cheap little snuff-boxes, buttons, and the like known to have been made in Birmingham before 1755 by John Taylor,[1] who in that year employed some five hundred persons, mostly for making buttons of various kinds. Taylor himself may well have been one of the pioneers in the manufacture of cheap enamelled bibelots. It is probable that he was established as an enameller before 1750. Not only was he fully equipped with the basic facilities for making the boxes and similar copper mounts, but he was also partner in a flint-glass works at Stourbridge.

William Hutton, a contemporary manufacturer well known to Taylor, in his *History of Birmingham* published in 1781, wrote:

> To this uncommon genius we owe the gilt button, the japanned and gilt snuff-boxes, with the numerous race of enamels. From the same fountain issued the painted snuff-box, at which one servant earned £3. 10. 0d. a week by painting them at a farthing each.

If such a painter worked a seven-day week and the fourteen-hour day of the period, this rate of production approximated thirty-five boxes an hour. Obviously this suggests that he must have employed an assistant, but even with such help his work at best must have been extremely crude.

It is probable that speedy production and incomplete understanding of the processes involved still resulted in enamels that soon flaked and chipped off the copper mounts so that few are encountered by present-day collectors. That Taylor himself was a successful man of business, unlikely to take up an enterprise which did not promise good results, may be gathered by the comment of James Watt to Matthew Boulton in 1775: 'John Taylor died the other day worth £200,000 without even doing one generous action'.

Taylor of Birmingham was by no means the only English enameller of the 1740's. In neighbouring Bilston the craft of japanning on metal had been established as early as the reign of Queen Anne, and it has now been confirmed that a group of enamellers from France, arriving in the town some time before 1745, taught what was hailed at the time as an improved art of

---

[1] 'Four Topographical Letters written in July 1555, upon a journey through Bedfordshire, etc., from a Gentleman in London to his brother and sister in Town, by R[esta] P[atching], 1757.'

decorating to the local japanners. At the same time, Bilston parish registers during the first half of the eighteenth century refer to a number of box-makers. Japanned snuff-boxes were certainly being made contemporaneously by John Baskerville in Birmingham, and it is exceedingly probable that the Bilston japanners turned out similar goods, using the local box-makers' products.

Here in Bilston, then, with the flint-glass centre of Stourbridge only a few miles to the south-west, was an obvious centre for anyone wishing to produce decorative enamels on a commercial scale and requiring boxes, mounts, enamels, and decorators. The period around 1740-50 has been ascribed with reasonable certainty to the rare circular patch- and snuff-boxes made of metal and often japanned, which have detachable lids bearing painted enamel plaques. These were probably Bilston products. Two examples are known to the authors bearing a close resemblance to the plated copper snuff-boxes made from about 1743 by Thomas Bolsover, the inventor of Sheffield plate.

As a point of interest, it may be mentioned in passing that the cottages where these French enamellers lived were only recently demolished. A probable reason for the migration of these craftsmen to England at this time, bringing with them a trade equally profitable in their own country, is some fifth-column association with the Stuart cause. Many agents are known to have established themselves in the Birmingham region, arranging for the delivery of arms and other insurrectionist material to strategic points throughout the country. Government forces captured considerable quantities of these Birmingham-made arms and accompanying Jacobite propaganda.

The manufacture of enamels having been already established in Birmingham and Bilston, it is probable that Battersea drew on this district for copper blanks and mounts. It is also probable that blanks already plainly enamelled were obtained from the Midlands for decoration in London. It is noteworthy that the two announcements of the bankruptcy sale at Battersea (see Chapter Three) fail to mention plant required for making enamel on a commercial scale. Several 'enamblers' at work in London during the 1750's have been traced by Mr A. J. Toppin.[1] These included Daniel Campbell, St Sepulchre, Middlesex, 1755-9; and Joseph Briddle, St Giles, Whitechapel, Samuel Smith, St Brides, and Joseph Pope, High Holborn, all 1753. These men could have been porcelain decorators. There is also the possibility that they were connected with the goldsmith's craft. A similar uncertainty attaches to Swift's reference in 1740 to 'enamelled silver plates to distinguish

[1] *Transactions of the English Ceramic Circle*, 1942.

38

bottles of wine by'. Joseph Allen, St Luke, Middlesex, was specifically recorded as a 'snuff box maker and Enameller' as early as 1742-54.

Nevertheless, in 1758, Dossie, in *The Handmaid to the Arts*, commented on 'the modern improvement in the art of enamelling'. He referred to the process as 'an art of late introduction amongst us', and spoke of the difficulty the English enamellers found in preparing their grounds, fluxes, and colours, these being a monopoly of Venice and Dresden. English enamellers, said Dossie, were

> for the most part obliged to employ a white enamel prepared at Venice for their ground, to pick up the remains of a kind of glass [opaque white] formerly made there, for a flux, and to procure their colours in a more perfect or faulty state as they can meet with them, except in the case of those who have recipes for some kind which they can prepare ...

> The art of enamelling has become a basis of a manufacture from which we may expect great advantages; since we already see it carried suddenly to such a degree of perfection, with respect to the facility of working, as to raise a demand for the produce in the foreign markets.

This, written within two or three years of the closing of Battersea, is clear contemporary evidence that Janssen's productions had revolutionized the trade in painted enamels. It also indicates that fine enamels were being produced in England at a price low enough to compete with the painted enamels of Geneva, where Petitot had been enamelling watch-cases and the like well over a century before, and the traditional skills of the town might have been expected to ensure continued supremacy.

Chapter Three

YORK HOUSE, BATTERSEA
1753-6

IMPORTANT as it is to acknowledge the existence of English painted enamels of the 1740's, it must be admitted that they appear to have been of little intrinsic value. It was not until late in 1753 that a new chapter opened in the story of the enameller's ancient craft. Only then did English painted enamels make any considerable claim to lasting appreciation and a place among this country's treasury of minor decorative arts. The production of Battersea enamels lasted less than three years. Yet 'Battersea' has remained the one title of distinction ever since. South Staffordshire and Birmingham produced many more ornate pieces, more technically brilliant, and with a greater range and delicacy of colour. As 'toys' these products may well have appeared in contemporary eyes as more gaily and appropriately decorative. Yet, reviewed today, Battersea productions stand out from the rest, distinguished by an exclusive quality of artistic worth, such as might be expected of that picturesque personality, the friend and associate of the leading artists and engravers, Stephen Theodore Janssen.

Indeed, it seems obvious enough that Janssen would never have been persuaded to launch the Battersea project had he not been convinced that it offered an opportunity to present, at highly competitive prices, the work of such really notable engravers as Simon-François Ravenet on the trinkets of the day for which the market seemed assured. As a prominent merchant-stationer, he was wholly familiar with the processes of engraving and printing, and doubtless in a favourable position to acquire the delicate glazed transfer paper,

15. A brilliant example of a painted casket, the lid measuring 8 × 5 inches.   The Italian Comedy subject is taken from Antoine Watteau's painting *Pour garder l'honneur d'une belle . . . c'est trop peu de Pierrot pour faire sentinelle.* Inside the lid is a dainty painting of two birds. The superbly painted flowers and insects on the sides of the box are shown in greater detail in the lower photograph.

41

16. The lid and interior of a box partitioned for ink and pens, and measuring $7\frac{1}{4} \times 4\frac{3}{4} \times 2$ inches. Such crowded harbour scenes later tended to give place to pastoral views enclosed in scrollwork.

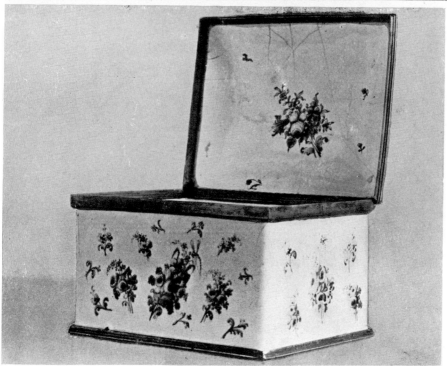

17. Another box lid painted all over with an individualistic Venetian scene. As in the previous example the minor decoration suggests the porcelain decorator's technique.

18. The lid, measuring $8\frac{1}{4} \times 5\frac{1}{2}$ inches, of a box decorated in vivid, clear tones of blue, pink, yellow, and so on. An individualistic piece of work showing enamel painting at its best before speed of production became all-essential. The sides carry separate posies of flowers, with formal purple ornament at the corners, and more flowers decorate the base.

44

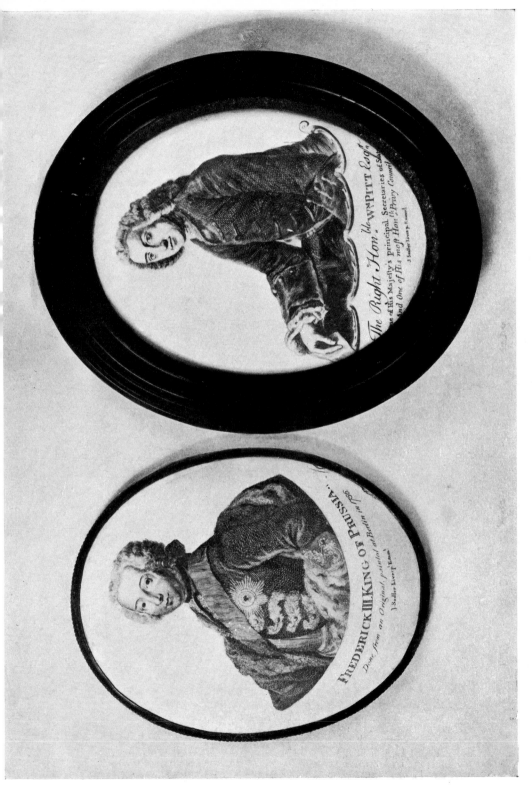

19. Two plaques clearly printed in black, their maximum diameters $5\frac{7}{8} \times 4\frac{3}{4}$ inches. These were made by John Sadler, the Liverpool enameller, and their inscriptions assist in their dating. The print of Frederick III, King of Prussia, is self-explanatory. That of William Pitt, later Earl of Chatham (1708–78), is copied from an engraving by Richard Houston of a painting by William Hoare now in the National Portrait Gallery, and the wording shows that the enamel was issued between his appointment as Secretary of State in 1756 and his resignation in 1761.

20. A vividly painted plaque measuring 8 × 6 inches. The dress of all the figures is in clear light colours —yellow, green, red, blue, mauve—standing out brilliantly against the stippling of the background. The subject is a much simplified and modified form of Watteau's *L'Amour au Théâtre Français* (1734).

21. The companion plaque to Number 20. Here, too, an exceptional elaboration and delicacy of detail is found in the wooded background to the gay figures. The colours and texture of the foliage are particularly notable and indicate perfect mastery of the enameller's technique.

22. *Above:* A tiny medallion, $2 \times 1\frac{1}{2}$ inches, painted in rich colours with a miniaturist's technique. This is one of the comparatively few specimens of English enamels which carries a name and date, being apparently signed on the back '*Jean Mussard à Londres 1760*'. The scene is taken from a Daullé engraving of a Greek woman by Joseph Vernet.

23. *Left and top left:* Two shell-shaped boxes of notable workmanship showing the early style of all-over lid painting coupled with ornate flowers and fruit on the sides. Both have minor paintings on their bases. The lid subjects are taken from *La Partie Carrée* by Watteau (painted 1731), and *L'Après–Diner* engraved by de Larmessin after Lancret. Colours are bright, with particular emphasis on yellows and reds over red-brown outlines.

24. A snuff-box measuring $3\frac{1}{4} \times 2\frac{3}{8} \times 1\frac{3}{8}$ inches which can be dated exactly as it commemorates the marriage of George III and Queen Charlotte in 1761 (see page 81). Inside the lid is a companion transfer-print of 'Q. Charlotte', both prints and those on the sides being in soft purple monochrome. The ground enamel is notably good. Scrolls in raised white surround the lid portrait and also the verse on the base.

where already the process was being used for printing linens. Writing from Delville on December 9, 1752, Mrs Delany mentioned a visit 'to Drumcondra, half a mile off, to see a new manufactory that is set up there, of printed linen done by *copper-plates*; they are excessive pretty...'[1]

The basic method of printing direct on flat earthenware, such as tiles, had already been under consideration. Twenty years later, in 1773, Benjamin Franklin wrote to some unknown person:

> I was much pleased with the specimens you so kindly sent me of your new art of engraving. That on the china is admirable. I know not who pretends to that [invention] of copper-plate engraving for earthenware, and I am not disposed to contest the honor with anybody, as the improvement in taking impressions not directly from the plate, but from printed paper, applicable by that means to other than flat forms, is far beyond my first idea. But I have reason to apprehend that I might have given the hint on which the improvement was made; for more than twenty years since, I wrote to Dr Mitchell from America, proposing to him the printing of square tiles for ornamenting chimneys, from copper plates, describing the manner in which I thought it to be done. Dr Mitchell wrote me that he had communicated my scheme to several artists in the earthen way about London, who rejected it as impracticable.

It was obvious that technical difficulties would preclude the possibility of transferring clear-cut impressions from copper-plates direct to earthenware. John Brooks's successful idea was to convey the decoration from the copper-plate on suitable paper. But he was still confronted with the problem of finding a printing ink capable of withstanding the heat of a firing furnace. Experiments in this direction brought him into contact with Henry Delamain, a manufacturer of delft ware and a fellow-citizen of Dublin. To Delamain belongs credit for overcoming the particular technical difficulties involved in the application of these printed transfers to the normal processes of manufacturing decorated earthenware. It may be assumed that the first success of the Brooks-Delamain partnership was printing on flat tiles: Henry Delamain claimed in 1753 that 'he had purchased the art of printing earthenware with as much beauty, strong impression, and despatch as can be done on paper'.

This infers that the idea of transferring pictures to enamels had not yet

---

[1] *The Autobiography and Correspondence of Mary Granville, Mrs Delany*, vol. iii, edited by Lady Llanover.

been mooted. Indeed there are some grounds for the contention that the Battersea project was founded with the idea of decorating tiles and not enamels at all. The sale notice of 1756 refers to 'Dutch tiles, printed and plain'. Decorated earthenware tiles made in England had long been known as Dutch tiles. Even at the beginning of the century they were always so described by Daniel Defoe in reference to the production of his London tile works. Obviously it was to such tiles that Doctor Richard Pococke, Bishop of Meath, referred when he wrote from Knole in August 1754: 'From London I went to see the china and enamel factory at York House, Battersea'. Doctor Pococke's editors emphasize that his 'observations are unimpeachable', and in the past his statement has confused those who sought in vain for any records of porcelain production at Battersea.

The invention of transfer-printing on tiles has been claimed on behalf of John Sadler of Liverpool. It is important to note, therefore, that it was not until nearly two months after the second Janssen sale that Sadler and Green, the Liverpool potters, introduced their transfer-printed tiles. On July 27, 1756, the partners announced that, unaided, they 'did print 1200 earthenware tiles of different patterns in one day', which 'is more than 100 good workmen could have done in the same space of time by the usual painting with a pencil'. It seems probable that Sadler and Green bought the tile-printing equipment together with the original copper-plates at the Battersea sale, and operated it at their own works. It is possible that they also acquired some of the enamelling plant, for the *Liverpool Advertiser*, dated February 11, 1757, recorded that 'the curious art of printing from copper-plates upon Porcelain, Enamels and Earthenware, as lately practised at Chelsea [?], Birmingham and other places', was being carried on in the town. The purchase of Battersea copper-plates by Sadler and Green would account for many resemblances of design. Some printed transfer designs now attributed to Liverpool may well be of Battersea origin.

The undisputed Liverpool plaques, transfer-printed in black on strong white enamel, that bear Sadler's name, closely post-date the Battersea venture. That of Frederick III, King of Prussia, claims to have been 'Done from an Original, painted at Berlin in 1756', and that of William Pitt when he was 'one of his Majesty's principal Secretaries of State'—that is to say, between 1756 and 1761 (Plate 19). There is here a further possible line of enquiry based on the tentative theory that the familiar large plaques of the famous Gunning sisters, generally placed as Battersea work, are Liverpool products.

The large plaques measure $5\frac{1}{2} \times 4\frac{5}{16}$ inches, are printed in black, and show considerable stylistic resemblance to those of Frederick and Pitt. Although, of course, originating in the same portraits by Francis Cotes, they differ slightly in detail from the familiar transfer-prints in indigo and other Battersea colours found on smaller plaques, approximately $2\frac{3}{4} \times 3\frac{1}{2}$ inches, and in association with Ravenet prints on snuff-boxes assumed to be Battersea work. By degrees, however, more and more additional enamellers are being discovered. There are several other large oval plaques notably well printed in black from excellent engravings in the Ionides and Schreiber collections. Jet-black enamel is rarely associated with Battersea, but it appears probable that Delamain overcame the particular difficulties involved and that the engraver Robert Hancock thereupon suggested its notably clear effects for use with the transfer engravings he made for Worcester porcelain.

To return to the Battersea enterprise, it seems evident that Brooks and Delamain persuaded Janssen to finance their transfer-printing project and that the method proved sufficiently successful to be applied to both tiles and enamels. The stationer Janssen, impressed by the popularity of expensive painted enamels from the Continent, started his factory in the belief that transfer-printing would enable him to produce equally effective work at much lower cost. Even so, he set a very high standard for the artists and engravers he employed. If in reality his bankruptcy was due to the failure of this venture, it may be attributed to the fact that Brooks himself proved an unreliable character, prone to neglect his duties during the vital first months at York House.[1]

It has been suggested that Brooks endeavoured to continue producing decorated enamels after parting from Janssen early in 1754. It has even been mentioned that he may have continued the Battersea venture at York House after the bankruptcy sale. No evidence is as yet forthcoming in support of either of these suggestions, however, and *The Gentleman's Magazine* reported that in February 1756, two weeks after Janssen, Brooks himself was declared bankrupt. He was later reported to be continuing his disreputable ways in the Midlands and died at Chester in about 1780. The third associate in the venture, Henry Delamain, died in Dublin in January 1757.

Some enamels found today do bear portraits of a Mrs Brooks—sometimes erroneously referred to as Miss Brooks—copied from Richard Houston's engraving after the painting by Thomas Worlidge (reproduced in the *Connoisseur*, January 1924). This is now generally assumed to have been

[1] *Dictionary of Irish Artists*, by Walter G. Strickland.

the engraver's wife, a likely subject for the graver of Brooks's pupil Houston. This appears the more probable in that the obvious alternative, the actress of that name, made her first London stage appearance as late as 1786. But there is no reason to associate Brooks with the appearance of these transfer-prints, thickly over-painted in South Staffordshire style, since portraits taken from such notable paintings of the day as were available on prints were a feature of enamels for many years.

One point is directly accountable to the early association of the two Dublin men Brooks and Delamain with the Battersea project. Not only are the famous Irish beauties Maria and Elizabeth Gunning portrayed on many enamels (Plate 2), but their portraits may be accompanied, as in an example in the Ionides collection, by such delicate and appropriately complimentary Ravenet engravings as that of Paris awarding the apple to Hibernia under the approving eye of Britannia (Plate 7), almost certainly from an original by another Irishman, James Gwim (see page 74). This subject reappears on South Staffordshire work (Plate 7). Doubtless, too, these Irishmen were responsible for the production of the series of Battersea enamels depicting scenes from the Passion of Christ, taken from the engravings of the Frenchman Sébastien le Clerc the elder (d. 1714) (Plates 8 and 10). A series of plaques of saints, such as the St James of Compostella in Ravenet style in the Ionides collection (Plate 9), has also been ascribed to Battersea. In Ireland, as throughout Europe, various types of enamelling had been associated for centuries with articles designed for church use.

Despite the assistance of such pointers, however, it remains difficult enough to build up a full and accurate picture of the brief Battersea venture. From among so little contemporary evidence and so much subsequent confusion, it is necessary to decide what may be defined, with any certainty, as a Battersea enamel.

In the first place, it must be re-emphasized that undoubtedly Battersea's principal contribution to the enamel trade—and from Battersea to the whole world of ceramics—was the introduction of transfer-printing. Horace Walpole appreciated this, and in the earliest literary reference to Battersea enamels yet discovered, a letter dated Strawberry Hill, September 18, 1755, to his friend Richard Bentley, he wrote: 'I shall send you a trifling snuff-box, only as a sample of the new manufacture at Battersea, which is done with copper-plates'.

In his description of the villa at Strawberry Hill, 1784, Walpole lists among the contents of his china room 'George II and Frederic, Prince of Wales in Battersea Enamel', and, in describing the green closet, 'a king-fisher and ducks of the Battersea enamel: it was a manufacture stamped with a copper-plate supported by Alderman Janssen, but failed'. Apart from the Walpole references, mention of enamels is disappointingly absent from contemporary reminiscences and letters of the period, which could scarcely have been the case had production amounted to even a fraction of the quantity of so-called 'Battersea' found in the shops today. Even accepting the fact that the remaining pieces of Battersea appear to be experienced work, that there is no indication of a slow process of trial-and-error—in itself some corroboration of the fact that painted enamels were a considerable production before Battersea started—the number made there in less than three years can bear no comparison with the many hundreds of thousands made in South Staffordshire, Birmingham, and elsewhere.

Marks were never applied to English enamels in the way that trade-marks were to contemporary porcelain. The names occasionally found inside boxes generally appear to denote their owners. It is only rarely possible, therefore, to be positive in assigning a piece to an individual manufacturer. But at least some distinctions may be drawn between Battersea products and those of the 1760's and later so often attributed to York House.

So many different types of article have been ascribed to Battersea that it is necessary first to determine, as far as possible, the limits of the factory's production. In both the Janssen sale notices specific mention is made of enamelled pictures, snuff-boxes, watch-cases, and bottle-tickets, and in one there is further detail of toothpick-cases, coat and sleeve buttons, crosses, and 'other curiosities' which one must assume to have been very minor trifles. Conspicuously absent is all reference to more elaborate pieces such as candlesticks, hot-water jugs, and even to étuis and scent bottles, such as were produced in South Staffordshire. Diminutive scent bottles, shaped as figures in the Dresden manner, were certainly made of porcelain in nearby Chelsea, but not until at least three years after Battersea had closed, and enamels of similar style can only be accepted as contemporary with, or later than, these. In many instances the design of such porcelain bottles included a separate hollow base forming a patch-box and covered with a decorated enamel lid.

There is also reason, on technical grounds, for discounting the assignment of a Battersea origin to the small and often extremely well-coloured boxes modelled in relief in the form of birds, animals, fruits, and so on, in direct imitation of Dresden bonbonnières. None of the many examples inspected by the authors appears to have been made before 1765.

This still leaves undisputed a brilliant collection of Battersea monochrome transfer-printed work, in mauve, brick-red, crimson, and near-black. These transfer-prints may be classified in detail according to subsequent treatment. Some, such as the scenes from the Passion of Christ in the Ionides collection, were fully but not heavily coloured; considerable detail, not engraved, might then be added by the colourist. Some, like the youthful 'Prince George' in the collection of the late Queen Mary (Plate 1), were but lightly touched up with pencil brush-work in the same shade as the transfer. Very many other transfers were apparently left without subsequent tinting. They were notably clear-cut and evenly printed, the original engravings obviously made by men who were highly experienced and had leisure for careful, detailed work. A master engraver would make only an original copper-plate which would then be copied by apprentices and other lesser men. The flowing, slightly effeminate, but wholly graceful and decorative style of Simon-François Ravenet is particularly prominent in Battersea work (see pages 63–4).

For their subjects these engravers most frequently turned to the popular prints of the period. Portraits of royalty and other notabilities were executed with masterly precision of line. Transfers from the same plates were applied to plaques and to such articles as snuff-boxes; the reverse of a snuff-box lid might be given another print, not necessarily associated with that on the front. On the sides of the box, and perhaps on the base, might appear painted flowers or such recurrent printed motifs as Ravenet's groups of cupids representing the arts—typical of French work of the period. These were so popular that they reappeared in a poorer style on later Staffordshire work.

A certain number of these decorations have been established indubitably as Battersea work, and some have helped in the identification of others. Among these are several finely executed plaques of royalty. A notable example is the wistful little study of the future George III as a boy, taken from the mezzotint engraving by Ravenet dated 1751, which was part of a picture painted by Richard Wilson in 1749, and now in the National Gallery. Ravenet reversed the figure and added the ribbon and star of the Garter to his version. This is a rare enamel, but recent copies exist. Ravenet also engraved a portrait of George II. The well-known medallion of William Augustus, Duke of Cumberland (1721–65), a profile bust printed in crimson

I. Three notable miniature medallions. Those of King George III and Queen Charlotte are slightly convex, their maximum dimensions $3\frac{3}{8}$ and $4\frac{3}{8}$ inches. They are taken from the paintings by Thomas Frye engraved by his pupil W. Pether. The workmanship is that of a highly expert miniaturist with a delicate stipple technique. Below is a portrait of William Augustus, Duke of Cumberland, third son of George II. This shows an entirely different technique. It is taken from an earlier engraving by Ravenet. but is in the glossy, press-embossed style found on the boxes illustrated in Plate 68.

in which the Duke wears an ermine cloak over armour, is justifiably cata-
logued as a Battersea piece in the Schreiber collection, Victoria and Albert
Museum, but not all his likenesses are Battersea work. Some plaques taken
from the same source appear in the distinctive, highly coloured, highly embossed
and glossy style of one of the South Staffordshire factories.

The familiar plaque designed by L. P. Boitard, relating to the Free British
Fishery Society, has been established as Battersea work for a short-lived
society in which Janssen played a leading part. This opens up interesting
possibilities, for the style and execution do not suggest the mature work of
Ravenet, and at the same time they bear a close resemblance to those of another
enamel, a representation of Watteau's *Fêtes Champêtres*, engraved by Laurent
Cars (1699–1771) under the title *Fêtes Vénitiennes*, printed in soft red and
over-painted in the same range of translucent colours. In each enamel the
painter has added a foreground decoration, to fill in the remaining space,
consisting of two swans between clumps of water plants.

A plaque in the Ionides collection of 'The Fortune Teller', with a
similar type of foreground and the same over-painter's rendering of swans,
is taken from one of six prints in an album in the British Museum discovered
in 1932 by the late Mr H. W. Hughes, and containing Robert Hancock's
earliest authenticated work. Designed by L. P. Boitard and engraved by
Hancock, three of these prints bear Hancock's signature. The names by
which the other five are known are: 'Peeping Tom', 'The Round Game',
'The Shepherd Lovers', 'The Singing Lesson', and 'The Pledge'. It must
be stressed that these designs, taken from other sources, appear on both
porcelain and enamels. The fact that an enamel carries one of these designs
is no proof of Battersea manufacture. But they do at least assist in the at-
tribution of the undoubted Battersea plaque of the British Fishery Society
as Hancock's early work.

Hancock's association with York House will be considered on a later
page. The immediate problem raised by the association of the British
Fishery and *Fêtes Vénitiennes* plaques concerns the number of other Watteau-
esque enamels that may have originated at Battersea as distinct from those
that are more probably later pieces. In this connection the size of some
pieces, generally attributed to Battersea, may be important. The British
Fishery plaque in the Schreiber collection and the associated version of the
Fêtes Vénitiennes both measure approximately $3\frac{3}{4} \times 4\frac{1}{4}$ inches ($3\frac{1}{4} \times 4\frac{1}{2}$ inches
in monochrome versions). A notably handsome casket in the same collection,

generally attributed to Battersea, has a lid measuring $7\frac{1}{2} \times 5$ inches—approximately the size of two such plaques placed side by side. Moreover, the design on this casket consists of an alignment of two Watteau subjects taken from his *Fêtes Champêtres* and his *Cascade*. Accepting the likelihood that Hancock was responsible for the engravings used for these transfer-prints, and even that they may have constituted early work, well within the Battersea period, it appears more than likely, nevertheless, that Battersea plaques and box lids kept more or less within the size range of the British Fishery plaques. Such handsome caskets may well have been made by a later firm from engravings bought at the Battersea sale, either by applying two transfers to the one casket lid or, in other cases, by considerable over-painting around a small central transfer.

This casket and others of a similar type, some bearing Italian harbour scenes in the Meissen manner, are decorated on the sides with elaborate naturalistic flower sprays wholly in the Chelsea-Meissen style. They lack the later gilded scrolling associated with South Staffordshire work and are a distinct individualistic contribution to enamel decoration. But their size, and the elaboration of their mounts, suggest their exclusion from the Battersea venture. In both Battersea sale notices snuff-boxes are specified, but nothing in the nature of a casket.

Again, in the Ionides collection there are such magnificent boxes and plaques as the box bearing a version of Watteau's *Pour garder l'honneur d'une belle . . . c'est trop peu de Pierrot pour faire sentinelle*. The box on which this appears (Plate 15) also seems to be a notably early piece, lacking the ornate rococo treatment general in later work, when the source of inspiration was Sèvres. Here, too, the sides of the box are ornamented with the heavy careful flowers and insects of the porcelain artists. These are far more detailed than most of the later flower sprays. About such work there can only be speculation. Such heavy flowers and delicate insects abound in the collection of decorative motifs by Jean Pillement and others entitled *The Ladies Amusement; or, Whole Art of Japanning Made Easy*, dating about 1760. Even such mannerisms as the pairs of swans associated with the painting over Hancock's prints are found, for instance, on the base of a later bonbonnière in the form of a swan. Indeed, Watteau's precursor in outdoor conversation pieces, Claude Simpol, introduced similar swans and reeds in the foreground of his picture *L'Isle de Cythère*.

That Watteau's subjects were not exclusive to Battersea is indicated by the appearance of his *L'Amour au Théâtre Français*, for instance, as the basis for a plaque in the Ionides collection (Plate 20) executed with opaque brilliance in an extremely individualistic style bearing no resemblance to any known work of Battersea.

As regards Hancock himself, there is evidence that his engravings were used at York House, and it appears likely, although not proved, that he worked there as a regular employee. The album of drawings already referred to was published for sale to decorators everywhere, priced at sixpence. All the patterns are shown in reverse, the figures all depicted as if left-handed. This permitted copying direct to the copper-plate, assisting speed of production by inexpensive pupil engravers not yet proficient in working in reverse.

Adaptations of 'Peeping Tom' appear on several enamels in the Ionides collection. A snuff-box, No. 13 in the Schreiber collection, shows this design printed in red and over-painted in colours. Hancock's design has been found to be adapted from an engraving by Jacques-Philippe Le Bas, after a painting by François Boucher entitled *Pensent-ils au Raisin?* Both painting and engraving are dated 1747. No. 4 in the Schreiber collection bears the same picture in red monochrome.

The enamels depicting the so-called 'Round Game', also directly associated with Hancock through this album, are particularly interesting. This picture, from *Le Jeu de Quatre-Coins* by Nicolas Lancret, engraved by Nicolas de Larmessin, is signed in script 'R.H.*Sc*' and 'R. Hancock *Sculp*' and was published 'according to Act 1754'. It appears on two vividly coloured plaques in the Ionides collection, with yet again two swans in the foreground. On a yellow box in the collection of the late Queen Mary, the print more closely resembles Hancock's original engraving and lacks the painted swans (Plate 12).

Regarding the other prints in this interesting little album, 'The Shepherd Lovers', signed in script 'Boitard *sculp*', is printed in brownish-purple on the lid of a Battersea enamel snuff-box, No. 14 in the Schreiber collection. Its origin has not yet been discovered, but the engraving does not suggest the hand of Hancock. 'The Singing Lesson' is signed 'Boitard *delin*' and 'Hancock *Sc*'. A section of this picture is applied to the side of a snuff-box in the Ionides collection in association with 'Parrot and Fruit', which appears under Hancock's signature in *The Ladies Amusement*. This book of patterns contains several which appear to be taken from engravings in use several years before the assumed date of its publication, 1760, so that it must be consulted with caution in any effort to establish post-Battersea work.

'The Pledge' is unsigned and appears to have been adapted from an engraving by George Bickham the map-engraver, in *The Musical Entertainment*, published 1738 by Charles Corbett, Fleet Street. This has not yet been noticed on enamels.

Experts are agreed that enamels bearing adaptations of these six small Hancock engravings, or details taken from them, may be of Battersea origin. They have also been noted on enamels of a considerably later date, on Bow and Worcester porcelain, and on Liverpool tiles. This is no indication, however, as to where Hancock himself was working when his copper-plates were in use.

For still further speculation as to possible Battersea and Hancock associations, there is, for example, one interesting little 'Jacobite' box in the Ionides collection. Here, inside the lid, is an obvious portrait of Prince Charles, in armour and with rays of light shining down upon him in benediction (Plate 27). The sides of the box have an 'early' treatment of flower groups, and on the outside of the lid is a conventional study of a man and woman talking, the man leaning elegantly against a fence. This bears a strong resemblance to other Hancock work. There is a somewhat similar group in *The Ladies Amusement*, and Mr Cyril Cook[1] has found a Worcester saucer and a Bow bowl which much more closely resemble this lid. But in neither treatment has the man the Jacobite white cockade in his hat, which is conspicuous in the Ionides enamel, and which suggests that the painter of the box, whether at Battersea or rather more probably at Bilston, wished to link the 'conventional' cover subject with his Jacobite hero within.

To return to more certain ground, it is important to note that none of the proven Battersea work bears any of the raised gilded rococo scrolling so decoratively conspicuous on later enamels. All pictures are carried out to the margins, if necessary by over-painting. Even the use by Battersea of flat, purple scrolling has not been proved. The portrait long thought to be of Janssen in which such scrolls appear has been identified by the Hon. Mrs Ionides as that of the Rt. Hon. William Beckford, when created Lord Mayor of London for the second time (1769), from an unsigned print made for Carington Bowles, St Paul's Churchyard. The enamel plaque in the collection of Her Majesty Queen Mary (Colour Plate I), of George I, after the portrait painted by Thomas Frye in 1761, and engraved by his pupil W. Pether, is found similarly surrounded with roughly painted scrolls.

Flat, scrolling rococo designs also enclose panels of fine trellis diaper

[1] *The Life and Work of Robert Hancock*, by Cyril Cook (Chapman and Hall, 1948).

printed in gold on some enamel boxes attributed to Battersea. This has worn badly, usually now showing little but a brown undertone. It would certainly seem to precede the more brilliant raised scrolls and diapers, and it appears in association with work in the styles of Ravenet and Hancock. A box with a Ravenet engraving of George II transfer-printed inside the lid carries elaborate shell and flower diaper in a reddish shade surrounded by flat scrolling in the same tone which may once have been gilded. The usual line-and-dot diapers and associated gilded scrolls on many good quality boxes and étuis obviously resulted from such early experiments.

The colours used for transfer-printing at the Battersea period were soft tones of red, sepia, purple, and indigo or purplish-black. All these inks, based on metallic oxides, had to be composed with a view not only to clarity of transfer outline but also to endurance of the subsequent firing process without spoiling. They were applied to copper-plates then lacking the later hardening treatment and therefore incapable of giving more than perhaps two hundred successful impressions on to thin transfer paper—itself probably the source of greater problems in the mid-eighteenth century than has been generally appreciated. The presence of the transfer base is often scarcely discernible when the work has been coloured by hand, however. This is particularly noticeable in post-Battersea work where heavy, opaque colours have been applied. The method of adding full-colour brush-work over a transfer base was a peculiarly English trait in decorative enamelling.

In the Battersea productions there is indication that the colour range was still somewhat limited. Generally it tended to be more delicately translucent than that on later work. Four clear, vivid colours are to be noted as particularly associated with York House: deep pink, blue, light yellow, and a reddish, dark brown, suggesting that subtler shades were still difficult to produce under the exacting conditions of the heat process. The well-known and comparatively crude plaque commemorating the Free British Fishery Society displays much the same range of tones as the totally different Passion series.

Such primary colours, however, are displayed to excellent advantage on the soft, creamy-white background of the true Battersea enamel. This enamel appears in several tones and surface qualities, indicating that even if a standard formula were used the materials themselves varied widely in quality. It was usually thick, with a brilliant sheen somewhat resembling soft paste porcelain. This was an excellent surface for the hand-painted decoration executed with the porcelain enameller's technique. The plaque of Prince George in Her

Majesty Queen Mary's collection shows the enamel still in perfect condition, with no trace of the disfiguration frequently apparent on later work. The colours melted over the enamel base delightfully, and transfer-printed lines adhered to its smooth surface with meticulous precision. The high but not glassy glaze of the white enamel on Battersea work is indication that tin still played an important part in its composition (see Chapter Six). Enamel of this high quality is only sometimes found on later work at a period when enamels were more usually opacified with arsenic and a high glaze produced by a film of flint-glass.

Various reasons relating to the methods of production at York House have been put forward to account for Janssen's bankruptcy in 1756, but there is no evidence that the enamel project precipitated this disaster, since Janssen was primarily a stationer living in St Paul's Churchyard. The first intimation of his financial difficulties was an advertisement relating not to York House but to his home. In the *Daily Advertiser*, February 28, 1756, appeared the announcement:

> To be sold by auction by Robert Heath, by Order of the Assignees, on Thursday next and the following days:
>
> The genuine Household Furniture, Plate, Linen, China and Books, of Stephen Theodore Janssen, Esq., at his House in St Paul's Churchyard. . . .
>
> Also a quantity of beautiful enamels, colour'd and uncolour'd, of the new manufactory carried on at York House at Battersea, and never yet exhibited to public view, consisting of Snuff-boxes of all sizes and of great variety of Patterns, of square and oval pictures of the Royal Family, History and other pleasing subjects, very popular ornaments for cabinets of the curious, Bottle tickets with chains for all sorts of liquor, and of different subjects, watch-cases, Toothpick-cases, Coat and Sleeve Buttons, Crosses and other Curiosities, mostly mounted in metal, double gilt.
>
> To be viewed from Monday next till the time of sale.
>
> Catalogues to be had . . . of Mr Chesson, Upholder in Fenchurch Street, Mr Humphreys, Upholder in St Paul's Churchyard and of Mr Heath, in Broad Court, Bow Street, Covent Garden.

These enamels were apparently Janssen's personal collection and would no doubt be pieces of the highest quality, perhaps specimen pieces since they are announced as 'never yet exhibited to public view'. This could not have been the case had his St Paul's Churchyard house been used in any way as a showroom or a City repository.

The story of dispersal is taken a stage further by an advertisement, discovered by William Chaffers in a source unstated, in the following June, announcing the sale of the stock-in-trade at York House:

> To be sold by auction by order of the assignees on Monday next, June 8, 1756, and the following days, at York Place, at Battersea, in Surrey—
>
> The household furniture and entire stock of STEPHEN THEODORE JANSSEN, Esq., consisting of a great variety of beautiful enamell'd pictures, snuff-boxes, watch-cases, bottle tickets, etc., great variety of blank enamels of various sizes, copper frames for mounting the unfinished enamels, with all the utensils, etc., belonging to the manufactory, also a great number of copper-plates, beautifully engraved by the best hands; some hundred dozens of stove plates and Dutch tiles, painted and plain, with many other particulars specified in the catalogues, which will be ready to be delivered at the House on Friday and Saturday next, the days of viewing, by T. Humphreys, Upholder, in St Paul's Churchyard, and by Mr Chesson, Upholder, in Fenchurch Street. The place is most pleasantly situated, with a convenient creek for barges and boats coming up to the house, which has been fitted up at a very great expense, with every conveniency for carrying on the said manufactory, which, if any person should think of continuing, they may be treated with by the assignees before the day of sale.

Apparently the goodwill was not disposed of, for the factory remained unoccupied after the end of June. Unfortunately no copy of the sale catalogue has been discovered. No doubt other enamellers of London, Birmingham, and South Staffordshire took advantage of the golden opportunity of inspecting their rival's equipment. Indeed, this dispersal of Battersea copper-plates accounts for many problems of similarity of design which have confronted collectors of both enamels and contemporary porcelain. The 'great variety of blank enamels' offered at the sale may account for the occasional discovery of an undoubted Battersea lid on a South Staffordshire box enamelled by a later process.

Of the men closely associated with Janssen in the Battersea venture, one of the most notable was Simon-François Ravenet (1706–74), an eminent pupil of J.-P. Le Bas, who produced many of the copper-plates for the Battersea transfer-prints. In view of Ravenet's status among artists it is unlikely that he engraved on the premises at York House. At his own studio he would employ a group of engravers engaged in copying copper-plates from his designs. Occasional Ravenet signatures have been noted. J. T. Smith in *Nollekens and His Times*, 1829, writes that 'Ravenet was employed to engrave copper-plates from which the articles were stamped, consisting of scrolls, foliage, shells, pastoral subjects, and figures of every description. Of some of these productions, I have seen impressions on paper, and they, as well as everything from the hand of Ravenet, do him great credit.'

This description does less than justice to his graceful, competent handling of portraits, contemporary groups, and illustrations of classical scenes. His religious subjects include 'The Holy Family', 'The Crucifixion', and several saints (Plate 9); among his many classical works appearing on enamels may be mentioned 'Danae and the Shower of Gold', 'The Metamorphosis of Clytie', 'Laocoön and the Wooden Horse' (Plate 6), 'Venus and Triton' (Plate 4), and 'Britannia presenting coins to Science and the Arts' (Plate 6). In addition to his engravings for plaques and boxes a number of Battersea bottle-tickets exist which are undoubtedly his work, showing the same sympathetic line work following and emphasizing the contours of the flesh and the flow of the draperies. These are in wavy escutcheon shape and measure about two and a half inches wide by two and a quarter inches deep. The most representative collection yet made was gathered together by the Hon. Mrs Ionides, who has presented them to the Victoria and Albert Museum. Dr N. M. Penzer[1], in a comprehensive chapter on Battersea enamel wine-labels, describes in detail Ravenet labels in nineteen different designs and inscribed with twenty-four names of wines. Some Chelsea porcelain bottles display a notable similarity of thought in associating cupids with a distillery.

Ravenet conscientiously decorated each wine-label with a transfer picture of cupids or *putti* engaged in work connected with the name on the label. These same transfers have been observed by Dr Penzer both outside and inside small Battersea boxes. In the Ionides collection is a snuff-box with a lid decorated on the outside with the 'claret' design and on the inside with that for 'mountain', in association with the 'burgundy' motif on the base of the box. These are replicas in reverse of the wine-labels, the copper-plates probably made by an apprentice not yet capable of working in reverse.

[1] *The Book of the Wine Label*, by N. M. Penzer (Home and Van Thal Ltd., 1948).

25. A cabinet in the Ionides collection indicating the range of objects made in painted enamels from hot-water jug to needle-box. The central plaques above the second shelf are noteworthy as examples of exceptionally rich black transfer-printing.

26. Interesting as an early example of what became a popular notion with the enamellers, this little box was obviously supplied to the purchaser with a blank reserve on which he had inscribed for him his name and the date. Later in the century many shops sold or gave away such boxes as souvenirs (see page 84). The box is a soft deep green, the flowers in full colours slightly raised.

27. Two boxes associated with Prince Charles Edward. The two illustrations on the left show exterior and interior of a notably well-painted box, the former suggesting Hancock's Worcester style. The man wears the white cockade, but the portrait of the Young Pretender himself is reserved for inside the lid, with rays of light shining down upon him. Side and base show brightly coloured flowers. The photograph below is of a tartan box. The lid exterior has a scene of figures and waterfall less expertly painted than the portrait inside the lid (illustrated here) which is after Tocqué.

28. A circular box, diameter 2½ inches, with a picture of Shakespeare and the words ANTE OMNIA MUSAE. This might perhaps have been issued in connection with the Shakespeare celebrations of 1769. The base shows a woman carrying garlands.

29. *Centre, right:* Nancy Dawson, the famous dancer who appeared at Sadlers Wells and Covent Garden, decorates the lid of this exceptionally lavish box. Her career ended in 1767 which suggests a fairly early origin for this specimen. The sides are of pinchbeck decorated in relief, with stags and swans between elaborate scrolling.

30. *Below:* Two views of a popular type of box. Although it measures only 3⅜ × 2¾ × 1½ inches, the top and base are neatly transfer-printed in black with the music and words of a *Gavotte* and an *Ariette*, the vertical sides with *Sig. Spurlettas Menuet* and *Lady Hardings Menuet*, and the ends with groups of music folios and playing cards. The delicate painting inside the lid appears to be executed over a transfer-print, ill-adapted to the shape of the box.

31. Three boxes, the largest measuring $8\frac{1}{2} \times 5\frac{1}{4} \times 3\frac{1}{2}$ inches, and the smallest $4\frac{1}{2} \times 3\frac{5}{8} \times 2\frac{5}{8}$ inches, all evidently produced when the craft in its second phase was at its best and success depended upon meticulous workmanship. The enamel ground, including the bases, is an extremely fine white exactly diapered in raised white dots. Raised gilded scrolls surround the carefully painted pastoral scenes which are in soft colours with considerable use of stippling. The mounts are very rich and bright, and the flat box (*top right*) measuring $6\frac{1}{4} \times 3\frac{1}{2} \times 1\frac{3}{4}$ inches, is fitted up in gilt metal for writing.

68

32. Five views of a tea-canister chosen to show the amount of careful work expended upon a single article, typical of good quality South Staffordshire work of around 1770. The turquoise-blue ground, diapered with raised white dots, is separated from the pictorial reserves by raised and gilded scrolling. The metal mounts consist of shoulder and base rims, the rim of the opening, and the matching edge to the exactly fitting lid.

69

33. The étui, about 4 inches high and fitted with tiny personal needs such as scissors and a slip of ivory for memoranda, was among the enameller's most popular products. These specimens display notably delicate metal mounts around top and base, and enriching the opening which comes between upper and lower decorated reserves. The ground colour is deep blue, gilded scrolls surrounding the flower posies and the scenes of fishing and dancing which are taken from the book of patterns entitled *The Ladies Amusement*.

34. Three étuis with finely tooled mounts. *Left:* An example in the highly embossed style. The whole étui is heart-shaped and the theme is continued in the hearts carried by the doves, and the cupids shooting their arrows at a target on a tree. *Centre:* The figure painting is taken from a popular print issued by R. Sayer of Lady Fenhoulet. The original portrait was painted by Reynolds and the mezzotint engraving made by R. Purcell. *Right:* Another popular subject on étuis — Mrs Brooks, from an engraving by R. Houston after Thomas Worlidge. In the original mezzotint the subject faces the other way and wears a patch on her cheek.

35. Less common designs for étuis included the book shape (*above left*) measuring $3\frac{1}{4} \times 1\frac{3}{4} \times \frac{3}{4}$ inches, with paintings on the 'covers' and raised white decoration on the back to suggest a leather binding. The 'page edges' are of bright gilt-metal and the top section of these slides off to enable the contents of the étui to be pushed up from below. The étui on the right, a cylinder 5 inches tall, has four tiny pastoral scenes among scrolls and flowers of raised gilt. The body unscrews near the centre to reveal knife, scissors and other typical étui equipment. These fit into slots around the central spyglass tube that runs the length of the article, the glasses at the ends covered by tiny metal slides.

36. *Below, left:* A writing-set fitted with pen, nibs, enamel-topped cut-glass containers for ink and pounce, and a fob-seal, accommodated in a slotted gilt-metal lining. The whole measures $2\frac{3}{4} \times 2\frac{3}{8} \times 1\frac{1}{2}$ inches. The background is turquoise blue with raised white diaper patterns and scattered flowers in gilt. The lid is painted with a pastoral scene.

37. Three interesting boxes of high quality enamel al with meticulously painted reserves set in background lavishly covered with gilt flowers and scrolls over deej blue. The top box measures $2\frac{1}{4} \times 1\frac{3}{4} \times 1\frac{1}{4}$ inches and has an inner lid of gilt-metal with a loop for holding a tiny gilt-metal snuff-spoon. The double box on the left has two lids hinged at the centre and a gilt-metal central partition. Except for the smooth white re serves, the sides of the box are corrugated. The mount are very rich: the decorative perforated rims ar soldered on and may have been an experiment prompte by contemporary methods on the Sheffield plate of th 1780's. The box to the right has a carefully execute portrait of William Pitt, Earl of Chatham, also illus trated in Plate 19.

38. A box of high quality enamel, of the same series a that with the portrait of the Earl of Chatham. Th portrait is that of George III, taken from a print issue when he was Prince of Wales.

Dr Penzer adds a warning: 'The term Battersea has been given to *all* enamel labels by the "trade", whatever the date, and although the expert collector is in no way deceived by such misapplied nomenclature, employed largely to create a market for the modern French and Belgian enamel wine-labels which just prior to the war flooded so many stores and "curiosity" shops both in England and America, it may well be that collectors of bottle-tickets are not so well informed'. Other wine-labels, many intended for sale abroad, were made later in South Staffordshire.

Some reference has been made already to the engravings by Robert Hancock (1730–1817) used at Battersea. Hancock was an eminent engraver of Staffordshire origin, and from 1772 to 1774 was a partner in the Worcester porcelain factory. He is considered by most authorities to have been employed as an engraver at Battersea throughout the period of its existence. This, although probable, has yet to be proved. Hancock was apprenticed to George Anderton, a minor Birmingham engraver, in January 1746, a fee of thirty pounds being paid[1]. A normal period of apprenticeship would have expired early in 1753, some months before York House was occupied. Even the appearance of Hancock's engravings on what are indisputably Battersea enamels, and in association with Ravenet engravings, cannot be regarded as proof that he was a regular employee there.

In Mr Cyril Cook's story of Hancock's life it is assumed that Hancock left Battersea for Bow, where he stayed for a few months, leaving for Worcester later in the same year, and thereupon introducing transfer-printing on Worcester porcelain. Regarding Bow, however, it appears more likely that Thomas Frye, himself an eminent mezzotint engraver, bought some of Janssen's copper-plates at the sale and used them for decorating his porcelain. This would account for the number of Hancock's designs found on Bow—more than he could possibly have produced during a six-month sojourn at the works. It is likely, however, that when Hancock left Battersea he settled in Birmingham as an engraver, and having already mastered the technique of engraving copper-plates for transfer work, offered his services to the enamel trade generally, locally and in South Staffordshire, as well as to Worcester and to Sadler and Green in Liverpool.

The rate levy books of Birmingham, 1763 to 1766 inclusive, show that a Robert Hancock was in business at 36 Walmer Lane. The Birmingham *Directory* shows him still at that address in 1770 and describes him as a

[1] *Transactions of the English Porcelain Circle*, A. J. Toppin (1932).

'toy-maker'. This was a trade description given to enamellers in contemporary directories, and it suggests that possibly Hancock the engraver was a maker and decorator of enamels even while engraving copper-plates for the Worcester porcelain factory.

That Hancock was well established as an engraver before 1760 is proved by the apprenticeship of Valentine Green, whose indentures to Hancock covered the period 1760 to 1764. Two other well-known engravers, James Ross and John Lowick, were apprenticed to Hancock in 1765, a fee of one hundred pounds being paid on behalf of the latter. Such a sum would not have been paid unless Hancock had by then become recognized as an engraver of considerable merit, well known and of some substance. It is not yet possible to prove Hancock's presence in Birmingham from the time he left Battersea until 1760. It is notable that several of Hancock's apprentices, such as James Ross and George Bothwell, eventually became prosperous copper-plate engravers for tranfer-printing in the Potteries, further proof that Hancock was an acknowledged master in this technical art.

A number of Sadler and Green tiles are decorated with transfer pictures taken from Hancock engravings. Similar designs have been noted on Worcester porcelain and on post-Battersea enamels. This again points to the possibility that, immediately after leaving Battersea, Hancock started in business as an engraver of copper-plates for transfer-printing, advising, too, on the technicalities of the factory processes.

In addition to engraving copper-plates for transfer-printing and his possible activities as a toy maker, Hancock engraved for book illustrations. Among these volumes was Valentine Green's *A Survey of Worcester*, published in 1764, and a *Life of Christ* by the Bishop of Down and Connor, printed in 1770 by Thomas Smith of Wolverhampton, whose presses were but three miles from the nearest Bilton enameller. It must remain a matter for speculation whether one of the Bilston enamellers for whom he was working introduced Hancock and Smith.

James Gwim (at work 1720–69) was another Irishman employed at Battersea, coming from Kildare, where he had been a coach painter. He is mentioned in the *History of the Professors of Painting in Ireland*, by John Williams (Anthony Pasquin), 1796, as arriving in London in 1755, where he 'got his livelihood by making designs for the lids of snuff-boxes, which he did for a manufactory at Battersea under the direction of Sir Stephen Janssen'.

A. J. Toppin has pointed out that Gwim specialized in mythological and allegorical subjects and that one subject found on transfer-printed Battersea enamels can be attributed to him. This—'Britannia Encouraging the Linen Manufacture in Ireland'—has been found, in the late F. C. Dyke's collection, with a contemporary inscription on the back stating that it was 'Drawn by Gwin, engraved by Ravenet for ye Battersea Manuf're under Sr J. Theodore Jansen, ye design a Compt for Linen Manufacturers of Ireland during ye Lieutenancy of ye Duke of Dorset'. This immediately suggests a Gwim origin for other subjects treated in a very similar manner, such as 'Paris Awarding the Apple to Hibernia' (Plate 7) and 'Britannia presenting coins to Science and the Arts' (Plate 6). Like Brooks, with whom he lodged for a time in Bloomsbury, Gwim was an eccentric. He was recorded in *Mortimer's Directory*, 1763, as 'Designer and History Painter, at Mr Rose's in the Broad Sanctuary, Westminster'.

James Banford (1724–87) has been traced by W. H. Tapp as a Battersea employee, who served his apprenticeship at Chelsea. He was a native of Clerkenwell and returned there later, working as an enameller under Thomas Hughes, junior. Tapp adds: 'I have little doubt that the well-known cut fruit and floral pieces, seen on Battersea enamels and Chelsea china, should be attributed to him'.

Another Battersea decorator was John Hall, whose entry in Bryan's *Dictionary of Painters and Engravers* reads: 'Hall was born at Wivenhoe, near Colchester, in 1739. He came to London at an early age and having exhibited considerable talent for drawing, was placed under the care of Ravenet, the engraver, with whom at the same time was W. W. Ryland. His first friends in London were Sir Stephen Theodore Janssen and Jonas Hanway.' J. T. Smith records that John Hall, 'when a lad, painted ornaments . . . under the direction of Sir Stephen Janssen', and this is confirmed by A. J. Toppin, who found that Hall was apprenticed on November 1, 1754, to 'Stephen Theodore Janson and Co., of Battersea, Surry, Toyman', for a fee of fifty pounds.[1]

Reference has been made already to other enamellers at work in London at this period. Doubtless they were quick to apply the transfer-printing method and probably acquired the engraved copper-plates, making their work difficult to distinguish from that of Battersea. *Mortimer's Directory* for 1763 refers to 'James Goddard, Enameller, Denmark Street, St Giles', stating 'the branch of Enamelling professed by the Artist is the painting in Enamel History, Figures and Flowers, on watch cases, Etwees, etc'. This is particularly

[1] *Transactions of the English Ceramic Circle*, A. J. Toppin (1932).

interesting in that one of the rare enamels bearing a name has that of 'Anth. Tregent in Denmark Street'. This piece in the Ionides collection is a small plaque decorated with an almanack entitled 'A New Year's Gift for 1759'. The transfer-print used for this is identical with that on a snuff-box in the same collection. It is thought that some of the boxes decorated with transfer-prints of music and some commemorating Frederick's taking of Breslau in 1757 may come from the same source. Both Anthony Tregent and Charles Fenn—whose butterfly and flower designs, engraved by Hancock, appeared in *The Ladies Amusement*—have been noted by A. J. Toppin in Battersea parish records, Tregent in 1752 and Fenn in 1753. Thomas Craft, known to have worked later for Bow, has been noted in Battersea records of baptisms in 1753–5.

A tiny medallion in the Ionides collection may well indicate the name of yet another decorator in London, for on the back, in very small lettering, are inscribed the words '*Jean Mussard à Londres* 1760'. The subject is taken from a Daullé engraving, 'La Grecque Sortant du Bain' (Plate 22).

Chapter Four

SOUTH STAFFORDSHIRE WORK: GENERAL CHARACTERISTICS

TECHNICALLY, Battersea enamels marked a profound advance in production methods, wholly in keeping with England's reputation for mechanical inventive genius. But stylistically their treatment mainly reflected cultivated French taste of the mid-eighteenth century. Their decoration was dominated by the engravings of Simon-François Ravenet and catered for a sophisticated enjoyment of gracefully illustrated classical lore, and a knowledgeable appreciation of high quality one-colour printing over enamel lustrously smooth and white. Other eighteenth-century enamellers undoubtedly regarded their products as infinitely more *chic*; yet today these have an enduring and endearing quality just because they are so inimitably English, because they reflect with such vivid naïveté the English tastes of their times.

For too long the enamels of Bilston and Birmingham have been dubbed inferior because critics have failed to appreciate that they were purposely quite different. As technical achievements the best of them were very good indeed: preference between the two styles of treatment must be established as a matter of personal taste. Radiant in truly beautiful shades of turquoise, green, rose-pink, and royal blue, often delicately and refreshingly, if unambitiously, painted, and mounted with the skill expected from the workshop of the world, South Staffordshire and Birmingham enamels offered the not-quite-so-rich a dazzling opportunity to mimic the airs and graces of the exclusive few.

This candle-bound age cried out for colour. Gilded mirrors glinted on the walls; imported lacquer cabinets were endlessly imitated in cheap, variously 'japanned' furniture and ornaments, much of it by amateurs; there was a rage for colouring engravings. But here was a chance to introduce colour into an endless variety of the smaller and more personal details of everyday existence. At a time when this country was developing fast, exporting eagerly, thrusting forward with the idea that life could be graciously decorative for the many instead of the fortunate few, it was not surprising that glitter proved as acceptable as gold, just as paste jewellery outrivalled precious stones. Between what is today regarded as undoubted Battersea and the products of South Staffordshire is a difference as fundamental as that between the chaste simplicity of a Chelsea goat-and-bee jug and the gay frivolity of a sprigged and garlanded shepherdess, perching provocatively on a gilded rococo scroll. Indeed, basically, both the porcelain and the enamels of the 1760's and the 1770's may equally be regarded as translations into the English vernacular of the ornate grandeur then beginning to capture the markets of the world for the state-subsidized manufactory of Sèvres.

Not until the late years of the eighteenth century did the enamelling trade tend to lose sight of this ideal and sacrifice quality of both design and execution in the cause of price-cutting speed. Between, say, 1760 and 1785, the enamellers of Bilston and Birmingham were responsible for very many enamel 'toys' of extremely high merit. Yet today the designation South Staffordshire, Bilston, or Birmingham is rarely used by dealers in connection with pieces offered for sale, since until recently these terms have been associated only with the coarser, cruder enamels made after 1780. Of some seventy examples noted in one day displayed in London, and labelled Battersea, not a single piece could have been made there.

It was indicated in Chapter Two that makers of enamelled toys were already recorded in Bilston before 1750 and in Birmingham before 1755. During the eighteenth century any small trinkets were called toys; the London trade cards abound with references. Two, in the collection of Sir Ambrose Heal, specifically mention 'enamelled toys'. It is known that some of the early Bilston enamellers, graduating from tiny workshops, became rich as a result of the demand for their wares. But just as all the best English decorated enamels were long regarded as being automatically of Battersea origin, so, more recently, there has been a tendency to give undue prominence to Bilston work. In considering the great majority of eighteenth-century enamels in existence today—that is to say, those which there is no reason to attribute to Battersea—the fact must be remembered that both Wednesbury, a mere two or three miles away, and Birmingham, just beyond the Staffordshire border, offered enamellers similar opportunities for manufacturing enamels on a large and profitable scale. Mounts, enamels, and practised craftsmen were equally available, and also the same tradition in skilled decorative work from associated employment on japanned ware and, in Wednesbury, on pottery. Much has still to be learnt of the trades of eighteenth-century Birmingham, but there is good reason to credit this city with the most ambitious enamel-work of the period.

As early as 1757 Bishop Pococke, writing from Wolverhampton, remarked that 'the people of Birmingham enamel in great perfection and cheap'. The largest of these early enamelling establishments was that of John Taylor (see page 37). As yet the style of his early decoration is unknown, but it is likely that he patronized Robert Hancock as an engraver of copper-plates for transfer-printing when the latter established himself in the Midlands. It is indicative of the town's potentialities for mid-eighteenth-century enamellers that by 1759, in Taylor's own words: 'There are two or three Drawing Schools established in Birmingham, for the Instruction of youth in the Arts of Designing and Drawing, and thirty or forty Frenchmen are constantly employed in Drawing and Designing'.[1] This is possibly the earliest instance of schools being established for industrial art in England and no doubt their existence had a profound effect on the enamel trade. In particular, it may well have helped Matthew Boulton to establish high standards of design and finish for the enamel-work executed in the Soho factory of Boulton and Fothergill, which was initiated in 1762.

What, then, may be regarded as the principal South Staffordshire and Birmingham contributions to English painted enamels? The plaques and boxes and minor 'curiosities' directly associated with Battersea were but a modest beginning. As technical problems were overcome and demand increased, pieces were produced in immense variety, including some of considerable size. Candlesticks were made at an early date, for in *Faulkner's Dublin Journal*, December 7, 1762, an advertisement appeared for 'imported enamelled candlesticks' offered for sale by 'Henry Clements in his toy shop, Crampton Court, Dublin'. This early type of candlestick followed the shape of early Georgian silver. Each was constructed in three segments joined by double-gilt mounts (Plate 76). Enamelling furnaces at this period were not large

[1] *Journal of the House of Commons* (1759).

enough to accommodate lengthy pieces, and the tall candlestick enamelled as a single entity may be dated later than about 1780. These tend to be clumsy looking, even when colour and decoration are good. Some are finely painted, but, in general, violent colour contrasts, rather than subtle harmonies, characterize such work.

Bearing in mind the fact that these enamellers followed, rather than created, styles of design, it is possible to give an approximate date for the introduction of other designs in imitation of silver pieces. Boxes of every size were supplemented by tea-canisters and caddy sets (Plates 32, 53, and 73); tobacco-presses, standishes, and their equipment for ink, shot, pounce, and wafers (Plate 78); cassolettes; counter trays (Plates 81 and 82); salts (Plate 80); mustard pots (Plate 48); cream jugs (Plate 74); and hot-water jugs (Plate 75).

Some of the trays bear evidence of having been quickly dipped in very liquid, milky enamel rather than coated in more viscid paste with a spatula, but many of the objects are extremely daintily finished. These vary from elaborate châtelaines to scent bottles in the form of billing doves, and heart-shaped étuis painted with cupids and their darts (Plates 67 and 34). Egg-shaped nutmeg holders, fitted with graters for their customary use with wine, hand-made thimbles drilled from the solid metal, cases for the hairpins then known as bodkins, toothpick-cases, even counters in the form of tiny enamelled 'playing cards', and innumerable other minor articles were added to the list. In the Ionides collection is a notable little globe (Plate 66) delightfully painted with figures representing the continents. The boxes with steel reducing mirrors of the 1770's were replaced by those with glass mirrors in the later 1780's, and from about 1780 date very many tea-caddies and tobacco-presses, as well as vast numbers of smaller articles extremely simply print-decorated. These included buttons, studs, brooches, breast-pins, watch dials, and end-pieces for curtain poles. The various styles of box with corrugated sides probably did not appear until the last years of the eighteenth century.

It seems likely that some large, handsome enamels in neo-classic style were the products of the firm of Boulton and Fothergill of Birmingham. In view of their dainty equipment and particularly finely tooled mounts edged with tiny flowers and scrolls, some little writing-sets and many étuis (Plates 36 and 33) may well be credited to the same famous firm (see Chapter Five). Designs for étuis included the book shape (Plate 35), with painted covers and a slide opening at the end, and the type in which the usual equipment of scissors and the like was fitted around a central spyglass. The Ionides

II. Two snuff-boxes and an étui with rich blue backgrounds. Typical in all essentials of good quality work of the later 1760's, these specimens have carefully painted panels, decorative flower details and an abundance of raised gilded scrolling in the rococo manner. The painted subjects are familiar on enamels, that on the central étui being perhaps the enameller's most popular decorative motif, a fishing scene taken from an unsigned engraving in the book of patterns of about 1760 entitled *The Ladies Amusement*. The box on the right has a version of a design by Anthony Walker which appeared in *The Compleat Drawing Book* (third edition 1762).

collection includes a travelling-clock made by G. Etherington of London, mounted in a turquoise-blue enamel case.

The Dresden bonbonnières in animal form appear to have been popular with the South Staffordshire enamellers when they began to seek novelties in the 1770's. The enamellers adopted Dresden ideas, already copied by Chelsea of the gold anchor period, and manufactured finely modelled boxes in the shape of human heads, birds, animals, fruit, etc. Usually the lid, forming the base of the piece, was painted with a suitably related subject. For example, in the magnificent Ionides collection of these bonbonnières, a box shaped and painted as a bird of prey, with another bird in its talons, has on the base a little painting of an agitated cock and hen protecting a family of chicks. These boxes would be among the 'new-fashioned enamel toys' mentioned on the trade cards of the period. They were reproduced more cheaply and in a poorer quality in the 1790's (see Chapter Six).

Bearing in mind the general change in taste, it is easy to distinguish comparatively early South Staffordshire and Birmingham work from the later, more ornate products. At first, in the Battersea style, the lids of enamelled boxes were usually covered entirely with pictures, and the white sides with prints or painted posies. Some elaborately mounted shell-shaped boxes, brightly but somewhat laboriously painted with subjects taken from such engravings as that by de Larmessin of Lancret's 'L'Après-Dîner', may be regarded as transition pieces. Then came a gradual development in the use of coloured backgrounds. When the coloured ground crept up on to the box lid some frame had to be given to the central decoration. At first this might be achieved with a few touches of flat gilding, which in turn gave place to more elaborate scrollwork in adaptation of the French *rocaille*. There was also a considerable output, mainly of boxes but also including scent bottles, étuis, plaques, and so on, in which parts of the design were considerably embossed and the painting applied to fit these shapings. Typical was the box with an embossed flower group, each petal of the central rose painted in detail. Slight embossing appears on a specimen in the Ionides collection which bears the date 1769 (Plate 26).

It seems to have been appreciated very early that decoration could be enhanced by the application of scrolls, simple flowers, and so on, in slightly raised enamel suggestive of iced decoration on a cake. This appears in white on a white ground surrounding a transfer-print of 'K GEORGE the IIId' on a box in the late Queen Mary's collection (Plate 24). Inside the lid is a print of

'Q. CHARLOTTE', and on the base, within further raised white scrolling, is Thomas Parnell's translation from *Pervigilium Veneris:*

Cras amet qui nunquam amavit . . .

translated as:

Let Him Love now
Who never lov'd before,
Let him who ever lov'd
Now love the more.

This inevitably suggests the marriage of George III and Charlotte and the date 1761. It was soon found that gilding applied to such raised scrolls was particularly effective. A massive box with Masonic emblems bordered with raised gilding in the Ionides collection is dated as early as 1764.

Thus, during the period of finest production in the Midlands, from the later 1760's till the early 1780's, a typical enamel box was a truly handsome piece. The mounts, of brilliant gilt metal, were finely tooled and fitted with carefully shaped lifters and perfect hinges. The outer surfaces of box and lid were richly or delicately coloured in royal blue or turquoise, pink or green, smoothly and meticulously applied. Superimposed upon this background colour there was often a raised diaper pattern of criss-crossed lines and interspersed dots in white or one or more harmonizing colours. In the collection of Her Majesty Queen Mary is a box of pink diapered in white, each square in the diaper containing a central dot of turquoise (Colour Plate III).

The slightly convex lid of the typical box was decorated with elaborate scrollwork applied in raised white enamel covered with gilding; sometimes this enclosed tiny flower posies painted in full colour on white reserves among the scrolls. The central white reserve of the lid was painted in full colour with or without the basis of a transfer print, and on each side of the box a white reserve among more gilded scrolling contained another tiny picture, painted in full colour, such as a figure group from *The Ladies Amusement,* or a simple flower posy. Sometimes the base carried another posy in colour or a single flower in gilt. A peculiar straggly gilt flower is probably the mark of an individual firm, and other base decorations which may eventually be identified include various simple dot-and-dash designs in raised white, applied like the diaper work on the rest of the box.

Such a box might be modified to suit individual requirements, with the inclusion of a personal portrait inside the lid or on a second, inner lid (Plate 60). More often, inside the lid, was one of the well-known portraits of the day taken from a popular engraving and coloured thickly over a transfer base which does not always entirely suit the shape and size of the space it has to fill. Other designs inside the lids were less conventional: the Ionides collection includes a painted lobster. Sometimes cracks in the enamel were ingeniously covered with paintings of flower sprays, insects, and so on, apparently at the time of manufacture.

All too obviously such lavish decoration lent itself to every kind of abuse, but this was largely confined to the later, hurried work. For instance, a speedier all-over decoration than the usual line-and-dot diaper was a meshed or netted background, either in white or in colour on a coloured ground which could be produced by applying a wash of colour over rather coarse muslin. This appears to have been a fairly early discovery of the Bickley firm, Bilston, and is found in the several colours used for background painting.

When over-painted, the network was covered by opaque enamels through which, in places, it might show faintly. For example, in the Ionides collection is a box with a blue meshed background. A medallion of green has been painted over this, surrounded by white scrolling, and against this green background is a coloured bouquet of flowers. This box has thus necessitated at least five firings: the white base, the blue mesh, the green ground of the reserve, the white for its surrounding scrolls, and the colours for the flower posy. Such an expense would not be undertaken by enamellers in a small way of business.

In dating enamels it is useful to remember the periods at which the different colours for backgrounds were introduced. Assuming that the South Staffordshire enamellers followed the obvious lead of the Chelsea porcelain factory in imitating the colours of Sèvres, it is valuable to note that dark blue first appeared there as a ground colour in about 1755; pea-green was mentioned in the sale catalogues in 1757; turquoise and claret colour were introduced in 1760; and silver, the rare yellow, and golden-reds from about 1770. English painted and printed enamels may also be found in lavender-blue, plum colour, brownish-olive, and especially in a pink or rose colour. This, known as *rose pompadour*, originated at Sèvres in 1757 and is not known to have been used in England much earlier than 1770. From about 1780 a chrome-tin pink was used in imitation. This was imported by Continental countries under the name of 'English Pink'. After about 1765 the white grounds of South Staffordshire enamels were harder and more glaringly white than formerly (see Chapter Six).

More formal background patterns included stars regularly scattered on a dark-blue ground, or in black over a yellow called *jaune jonquille;* netted purples and lavenders; and a marbled effect produced by mixing a strong colour in white.

The finest period for painted enamels covered scarcely thirty years. From about 1780, possibly earlier, painting tended to become less exquisite, gilding began to be applied carelessly, and the quality of transfer-printing deteriorated, as Bilston had to contend with the competitive mass-production methods developed in Birmingham and the establishment of the industry in nearby Wednesbury. Lower piece-work rates then compelled the decorators to scamp their work, although workmanship of the mounts and hinges was often excellent.

Typical of the mass-production work from South Staffordshire and Birmingham were the little boxes in dullish colours, usually oval, less well hinged and lacking base rims, which even at the time were regarded largely as souvenirs to be sold or given away at fashionable watering-places and holiday resorts. Many were printed with local views and the words 'A Trifle from'—London, Worcester, Margate, Tunbridge Wells, Evesham, Whitchurch, Dover, to name but a few. Some bore, in addition, painted in, the names of the shops that presented them to favoured customers, sometimes filled with snuff or face-powder. An American collector has accumulated more than four hundred different designs with such local associations. An example in the Ionides collection is dated as early as 1769, from 'Mich.' Knott, Rydal' (Plate 26).

For more general sale were boxes decorated with vacuous mottoes and sentiments such as 'Live and let live', 'The eyes have power to kill or cure', 'Trifles show respect'. Others again bore crude representations of current events, such as the series expressing thankfulness at George III's escape from attempted assassination, and those associated with the wedding of Queen Caroline. Whereas the later porcelain mugs and lucky pigs which replaced such mementoes were quickly broken, these have proved enduring and, unfortunately, by many they are still regarded as fully representative of the enamel-work of the towns that produced them.

Birmingham was, of course, the source of many mass-produced, shoddy enamels. 'A Trifle from Soho' is familiar among the cheap little boxes mentioned above, and is assumed to come from the Soho factory of Matthew Boulton. When in 1777 John Marston, brass-founder and toy maker, and Samuel Bellamy, die-sinker and engraver, patented a method of stamping hat- and cloak-pins, the enamel trade was immediately called upon to supply pictorial discs for these. The illustrations on page 144 show 'Cloakpins with enamel Pictures set in Stampt Metal rims burnish't of a fine gold colour', and also 'Enamel Chimney Piece Knobs'. These hitherto unpublished examples are from a priced pattern book issued about 1780. So far, these are the earliest known contemporary illustrations of enamels.

Such pieces had to be produced at highly competitive prices. They were transfer-printed and quickly dabbed with transparent colour. Some, like contemporary pieces stamped in brass in low relief, were given the simple 'classical' motifs then so prevalent, such as urns and vases. But some were rather more ambitiously decorated: the monstrous hats depicted in ladies' fashion plates of the day were particularly prominent on these cheap little objects. Others may be dated by their recording of topical events, such transfers being equally applicable to the souvenir snuff- and patch-boxes referred to above as products common to all the enamelling centres in the 1790's. The excitement occasioned by the 'air balloon', for example, prompted such a pictorial record. The same illustrations appear in pattern books nearly forty years later, proving the enormous popularity of such pieces.

Caskets made of iron, japanned in a rich shade of deep red, and patterned with gold lines, are sometimes found with their lids inset with high quality enamels, elaborately painted with the detailed Italian landscape and harbour scenes of the period. These have always been considered to be of Birmingham origin. There are about a dozen examples of these handsome and extremely interesting toilet caskets in the Ionides collection (Plate 71). After careful examination by the National Museum of Wales, the opinion has been reached that they were made at Pontypool.

This is confirmed by one of the patterns seen in the enamel surrounding the picture itself. One of the conspicuous stock designs peculiar to Pontypool japanned ware is an all-over meandering line known as the Stormont pattern. The enamel plaques of several toilet caskets have wide borders painted in flat gilt with this pattern. The general assumption that the firm of Boulton and Fothergill produced these enamels—no other Birmingham factory is known to have done enamel-work of this quality—is therefore open to question. Such an application of the Stormont pattern, not to the japanning of the caskets but to the enamel plaques upon their lids, suggests that there may possibly have been an enamel factory in existence in the Pontypool region.

The other well-established centre for decorative enamels in the late eighteenth century, however, was Wednesbury. Although but some three miles from Bilston, this town recorded no enamellers until 1776, and so far no enamels of proved Wednesbury origin have been indentified which compare with the high quality of the best from Bilston and Birmingham. Nevertheless, the town had the distinction of continuing in production for a few years after the last Bilston enameller had closed down.

Until the French Revolution in 1789 the majority of English enamels went abroad. They were exported principally to France and Italy, but in the Ionides collection is an English enamelled knife-sheath which has been mounted in China. The pale Oriental metal bears the mark of Ch'ien-Lung (Plate 47). Over-painted, transfer-printed decoration predominated in the export work to the Continent, its price being favourable in comparison with entirely hand-painted Continental productions. When Napoleon became all-powerful such English work was prohibited. Prussia imposed heavy duties, and after 1790 trade generally decreased so alarmingly that in 1793 England was faced with a commercial panic. For the enamel trade in particular the loss of foreign markets was felt the more acutely because the home trade was adversely affected by the high cost of copper. By the end of the century the majority of enamellers had been forced out of business.

Chapter Five

ENAMELLERS OF BILSTON, BIRMINGHAM, WEDNESBURY

INFORMATION regarding the various firms engaged in producing decorated enamels in the second half of the eighteenth century is still far from complete. Many of the most individualistic pieces were doubtless the work of small men employing only a few assistants before competition became too fierce for them. Nevertheless, some who started in a small way achieved such success that a certain number of facts concerning them have been established.

The earliest enameller of whom any personal record exists was Dovey Hawksford of Bilston. Francis Buckley found him described as an enameller in 1748, and referred to him as a toy maker to whom William Homer of Walsall was apprenticed in 1722. It is known that the young Homers eventually moved to the Bilston area and were engaged as painters in the enamel trade. The authors inspected a collection at Wolverhampton some years ago consisting of pieces painted by members of the Homer family for various factories in the trade.

As early as 1741 Hawksford was described as a chapman in a reference discovered by Buckley, and in the same year Benjamin Bickley, toy maker of Bilston, was recorded as accepting Joshua S. Devey as an apprentice—an engagement which had a sequel in the establishment later of the Devey family as toy makers in Wolverhampton, where they may have made mounts for the enamellers. Much more important to the present study of early Bilston enamellers, however, are Dovey Hawksford and Benjamin Bickley, the more so because there is reason for thinking that they were closely associated in the enamel trade.

Dovey Hawksford is known to have been buried at Bilston, March 31, 1749, and he was referred to in the news columns of *Aris's Birmingham Gazette* as having been an enameller. This fact must now be considered in conjunction with the knowledge that Benjamin Bickley was already established as an enameller in 1750. As early as 1729, on the occasion of his marriage, he was described as a toy maker. When Bickley died in 1776 he was succeeded by his son John, who died later in the same year. The Bickley enamel factory was then sold, being advertised in *Aris's Birmingham Gazette* on December 23 and 30, 1776. The announcement reads:

> To be sold, the stock-in-trade of Mr John Bickley, deceased, consisting of the tools and utensils necessary for carrying on the Enamel Business, together with the Stock-in-Hand (which is but small) of finished goods and unwrought materials, and also many valuable sets of patterns, now in the hands of some of the first Merchants in the Kingdom, from which considerable orders may be expected. For particulars enquire at his late dwelling house in Bilston.

The winding up of the estate disclosed remnants of a ninety-nine-year lease of which only twenty-eight years had run. The contract, therefore, must have been made in 1748, the year preceding Dovey Hawksford's death. Search through the *Gazette* has disclosed an advertisement of 1748 in which the land in question is described as covering eight acres

> whereon is erected a water-mill with two overshot wheels, 28-feet high, one part of which hath been used for grinding corn, and the other part is convenient for rolling any kind of metal, or boring of gunbarrels; there is sufficient room for fixing up spindles for a number of laps, which may be very convenient for several manufactures exclusive of a complete shop room for twenty pair of hands . . .
>
> Also to be sold at the same time and place, a pair of millstones, two mills for grinding enamels, a dressing mill, and several other instruments of a like kind.

The newspaper announcement does not disclose the trade formerly carried on, nor the name of the trader. The inclusion in the list of 'two mills for grinding enamels' is significant, however. To recapitulate: Dovey Hawks-

39. Two views of a fascinating little box inscribed inside the lid with the names of ten people who died between 1741 and 1763. The lid shows a wedding in a church and the base a funeral procession, while the sides carry scenes of everyday life.

40. A box showing advances in constructional technique which, as a memorial to David Garrick (the figures are shown tracing the words *Et in Arcadia Ego* on the tomb), may be dated approximately to 1779. The concave sides meet in fluted corners decorated with sprawling gilt flowers and the mount has an applied strip of hand-tooled ornament.

41. *Right:* Two boxes in the South Staffordshire or Birmingham manner painted with versions of popular French pictures. The first example shows much the same elaborate shaping as that in Plate 40 but is apparently painted by a different artist. The subject is Jean-Marc Nattier's *Les Amants* copied from an engraving of 1751 and found also on a painted enamel medallion in the Schreiber collection. The second box has its lid painted with a copy of Boucher's *La Courtisane Amoureuse.*

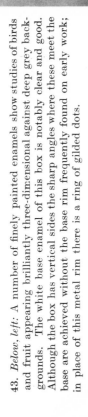
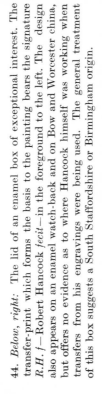

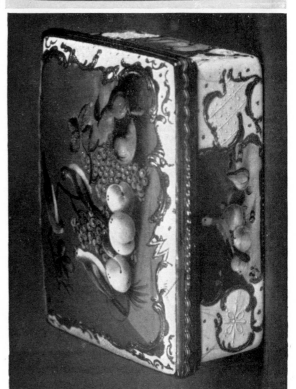

42. A snuff-box which has been given a tartan background to the usual conventional pictures on top and sides. Inside the lid is a painting of the Young Pretender.

43. *Below, left:* A number of finely painted enamels show studies of birds and fruit appearing brilliantly three-dimensional against deep grey backgrounds. The white base enamel of this box is notably clear and good. Although the box has vertical sides the sharp angles where these meet the base are achieved without the base rim frequently found on early work; in place of this metal rim there is a ring of gilded dots.

44. *Below, right:* The lid of an enamel box of exceptional interest. The transfer-print which forms the basis to the painting bears the signature *R.H. ƒ*—Robert Hancock *fecit*—in the foreground to the left. The design also appears on an enamel watch-back and on Bow and Worcester china, but offers no evidence as to where Hancock himself was working when transfers from his engravings were being used. The general treatment of this box suggests a South Staffordshire or Birmingham origin.

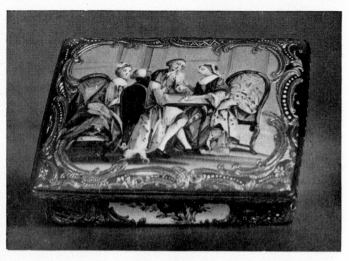

45. The soft-toned, liquid painting on this deep blue snuff-box lid may be compared with that on the box below. Inside the lid is a transfer-print of a youth talking to a milkmaid, copied from an engraving by Luke Sullivan, published 1759, 'A View of Woobourn in Surry, the seat of Philip Southcote Esq.'

46. Snuff-box with another painting of 'The Card Party', a subject sometimes attributed to the engraver Robert Hancock. Here a cleric forms one of the party. In the foreground a small dog barks at a cat on the chair.

47. A knife-sheath showing certain similarities of technique in both the main painting and the decorative diaper pattern, to the box illustrated in Plate 43. The interesting feature here, however, is the fact that the enamel has been mounted in China, the pale metal bearing the Ch'ien-Lung mark (1735–95).

48. *Top left:* Mustard pot of eighteenth-century enamelled ware with metal mounts to the lift-off lid which has a hole for a spoon. The ground colour is deep blue, the painting executed in full colour.

49. An étui pressed into an irregular shape which is emphasized by scrolling picked out with gilt. In its general treatment and paintings this suggests the same maker as the example on the left in Plate 34.

50. *Left:* Snuff-box with a lid painting of *Le Matin* from an original by Nicolas Lancret engraved by Nicolas de Larmessin. *Right:* A particularly dainty effect achieved by slight corrugations in this box.

51. *Left:* A box, 3⅜×2½×1½ inches, painted in an individualistic style with a candlelit scene reminiscent of the work of the Derby artist, Joseph Wright, A.R.A. The paper in the foreground begins 'Muttall Love' and ends 'Mad Tom'. The fishing group on the front is from the decorator's pattern book *The Ladies Amusement*.

52. *Right:* A deep box decorated in the popular Oriental style. Such designers as the Frenchman Jean Pillement, who worked in London, offered the decorator numerous themes of this kind. The man with two bells on a stick is a Pillement *motif*, but this box shows an unusual lack of invention, with details in the side decorations repeating those on the lid. The ground is white, decorated with raised white scrolls and dots, and the mount includes a particularly ornamental lifter soldered to the tooled ribbon of the rim.

53. A casket and one of the tea-canisters contained in it, illustrated to show the superb craftsmanship not only in the large surfaces of enamel composing the lid and sides but also in the chased gilt-metal mounts. Pastoral scenes and Italian landscapes by such painters as Claude and Boucher and such engravers as Vivares became the stock subjects with many enamel-makers and were produced in an infinite variety of pleasing if unexciting groupings.

54. A particularly ambitious specimen consisting of a knife and fork box in the style usually made of wood in the second half of the eighteenth century, with serpentine shaping, fluted corners, and exceptionally large surfaces of enamel. The minor decoration suggests recourse to *The Ladies Amusement*, and similar dainty flower sprays are painted on the enamel handles of the knives and forks fitting into slots inside.

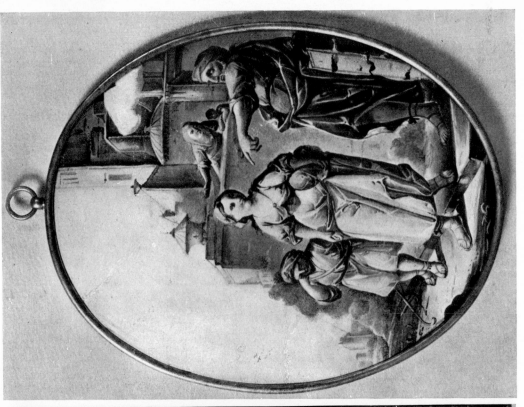

56. 'Abraham dismissing Hagar and Ishmael', a vivid, colourful subject originating with G. Zocchi, engraved by Joseph Wagner and used by such Dutch tile decorators as the younger Jan Aalis as well as the English enamellers, who supplied varying background details. The basic enamel in this plaque consists of a very thin layer of flawless white about 1/64th of an inch thick, over a thicker layer of white but coarser ground.

55. A plaque which is so much in the spirit of Hancock's work that one looks for a half-hidden signature among the foliage. In this specimen, however, the artist appears to have worked without the assistance of an underlying transfer-print. The subject is derived from one of the pattern books of the 1760's which reflected the Oriental taste for picturesque groups of exotic birds perfectly suited to the art of the enameller.

ford, enameller, died early in 1749, and in the previous year Benjamin Bickley acquired an already established enamel factory. And this was nearly five years before Janssen first occupied York House.

The output of this factory must already have been considerable to find use for two grinding mills, which, running a normal fourteen-hour day, would produce the material for enough enamel-making to occupy many 'pair of hands'. When founding a new trade the enameller would have been unlikely to equip himself with more than a single grinding mill: the introduction of a second suggests that he was well established, possibly the employer of those French enamellers known to be in Bilston by 1745 and mentioned in Chapter Two.

From the specimens that remain today, however, it seems clear that the main development of the Bilston enamelling trade dates from about 1760. At once it is necessary to reject the old idea of one or two individual enamellers whose hand may be detected in all the major South Staffordshire products. Enamelling was a craft, and one that flourished exceedingly in the second half of the eighteenth century. It has now been established that at least eighteen enamellers worked in Bilston. Local directory records tell their own tale of the rise and decline of the trade.

A descriptive note in the Bilston Art Gallery refers to James Brett of Bridge Street as an enameller in 1760, and lists as later rivals George Perry, Temple Street; J. Hoo Foster, Foster's Fold; S. Hanson, Swan Bank; E. Beckett, Bridge Street; Isaac Beckett, Duck Lane; Benjamin Bickley, and John Green. John Best (*d.* 1789) was another enameller and a well-known maker of mounts, fully established by 1770.

In addition to these, the Birmingham *Directory*, 1770, lists several other enamel box makers at Bilston: Isaac Smith, Perrey & Sons, Thomas Knowles, and John Buckley. John Perry is entered as an enamel painter; John Vardon as engraver and painter; John Green as a metal buckle maker and enameller —who is known to have made gilt metal mounts, too, for the enamellers. The *Directory* of 1781 lists only three makers of enamel boxes: Isaac Beckett, Widow Bickley, and Thomas Perry (*d.* 1808), in addition to John Green and John Vardon. The 1818 *Directory* contains four entries of enamellers: Edward Beckett, Bridge Street; George Perry, Temple Street, New Town; J. H. Foster, High Street; and Isaac Beckett. Edward Beckett is the only remaining enameller in the 1827 *Directory*, and in 1835 Susannah, his widow, is entered as an enamel box maker. Richard Askew, although recorded as a 'miniature painter' at his death in 1798 by *Aris's Birmingham Gazette*, may have worked as a decorator of enamels. He is well known for his decorative work on Derby china, in the style of contemporary enamels, but apparently left there in 1795 and moved to Bilston.

From among all these craftsmen, however, the Bickley family is as yet the one about which most details have been established. It was seen, in connection with the probable development of Dovey Hawksford's enamelling factory, that Benjamin Bickley acquired a well-established works in 1748. The 1748 advertisement regarding this factory mentions 'a watermill with two overshot wheels, 28-feet high'. This indicates a site bordering the deep stream which flows into Bilston from Ettingshall. The Bickley home was at Ettingshall Lodge and, as was usual with manufacturers of the period, adjoined the works.

When, twenty years later, the Birmingham-Wolverhampton canal was cut through Bilston, the Bickleys were proprietors of some one hundred acres of rich coal land, which at once became extremely valuable. They were quick to realize the potential profits to be secured and were the first to erect a blast furnace in Bilston. The Bickleys now became concerned in numerous financial enterprises, but in 1770 the Birmingham *Directory* described John Bickley as an enamel box maker and Benjamin as a toy maker: that is to say, a maker of various enamelled trinkets.

Mary, the widow of Benjamin, died in 1781 and she appears to have left her estate equally to John's widow, Catherine (*d.* 1814), who now became a wealthy woman, and to her half-brother, William. Her will also provided 'two guineas for mourning' for the enameller John Green.

A collection known to have originated in the Bickley factory was exhibited some years ago at the Wolverhampton Art Gallery and Museum. Various attempts have been made to distinguish this firm's products from those of other Bilston enamellers, but without much success. Even such a considerable matter as the use of a basic transfer-print as a guide to colouring the decoration is not easily settled: the general use of extremely opaque enamels for pictorial work was a notable Bilston divergence from the Battersea practice of applying thin washes of translucent colours.

One fact that may be remembered is that mirrors of glass in the lids of patch-boxes were not introduced until about 1785—after both Benjamin and John Bickley had died. Reducing mirrors of steel were occasionally used even after 1790.

William Chaffers, in his *Marks and Monograms on Pottery and Porcelain*, 1863, refers to the discovery of some 2000 enamels which had been stored for eighty years, suggesting that they came from the factory of George [James?] Brett, enameller of Bilston, from whom they had been accepted in lieu of rent.

The Brett origin of these enamels must now be discounted. Mr C. Clapham, of the Wolverhampton jewellery firm of Kemp and Wilcox, told the authors at the time of the Wolverhampton Exhibition that, as a youth, he well remembered the arrival of these enamels in several cases escorted by Mr Haden Corser, solicitor to the Bickley family. His impression in 1925 was that there had been many more than 2000 specimens, all in mint condition. The owner was a widow named Mrs Latty Bickley, wife of a grandson of John and Catherine Bickley. It was thought by Mrs Bickley that when the stock-in-trade was sold in 1776, the bidding for the small stock-in-hand failed to reach the reserve price and these pieces had lain forgotten in the attic of Ettingshall Lodge for nearly a century. Among these enamels Mr Clapham recollected a few candlesticks, many salt-cellars, several tea-caddies and numerous small boxes of all shapes. The candlesticks and salts had pink grounds and were decorated with flower sprays on white reserves.

Mr Clapham referred to the Kemp and Wilcox stock book which he wrote up in 1883, when only about a dozen boxes remained. About half of these were bought by Mr Joseph Jones, whose daughter, Mrs A. B. Bantock, inherited about twenty examples known to have been acquired from this source. Some of them are now in the Wolverhampton Museum. Some thirty examples from the collection of Mr Haden Corser and mostly acquired from Messrs Kemp and Wilcox were inspected by a relative of the authors in 1903. Again, the pink grounds were noted on a pair of candlesticks, and two pairs of three-legged salts. There were also three boxes in the forms of apples and a frog. Most notable, however, were two snuff-boxes of chased pinchbeck, their lids bearing painted enamel panels.

In 1871 Mrs Latty Bickley gave '18 small boxes and small articles in Bilston enamel', accompanied by a number of others on loan, to the South Kensington Museum. The latter were returned to her executors in 1897 and some were presented to the Bilston Museum.

If, indeed, these enamels were from the Bickley factory which closed in 1776, the presence of the pink background is evidence of this colour being in general use much earlier than has been supposed. The possibility must not be overlooked, however, that these Bickley enamels were productions from the factory of 'Widow Bickley, enamel box maker', noted in the 1781 *Directory*.

Another early Bilston enameller was Isaac Beckett (*d.* 1789), who appears to have been established in the trade by 1756. Beckett is known to have made considerable use of transfer-printing under the painted decoration. He originated the enamelled buckle and specialized in étuis. Isaac Beckett II (1756–1836) carried on his father's business from larger premises in Bridge Street. He was the uncle of Edward Beckett (1784–1831), the last of the Bilston enamellers. Benjamin Beckett (*d.* 1798), a brother of Isaac II, was a mount-turner.

F. W. Hackwood in *Wednesbury Workshops*, 1889, suggests that the secret of making 'enamel paste' died with Isaac II in 1836 and that an unnamed Wolverhampton japanner offered £1000 for this secret without response. So many people had been engaged in the trade that this seems unlikely. Hackwood may possibly have confused this with the offer of a similar sum by a Wolverhampton japanner for disclosure of the trade secrets used by the Allgood family at the Pontypool and Usk japan factories. This offer was made a few years after the closing of the Usk japan works in 1860.

It is as yet impossible to recognize, with any degree of accuracy, the enamels made at any particular Bilston factory. It is beyond question that some toy makers, now unknown, concentrated on making enamelled boxes, sending them out to specialist firms for decoration by hand or by transfer, and receiving them back for mounting and finishing. At the same time, an alternative arrangement was for a mount-maker to buy finely decorated lids of high quality enamel from one supplier, and second-rate bodies from another, and fit these together for sale at various prices. Boxes in which the basic white enamels of body and lid bear no resemblance to each other are frequently found.

As regards the decoration of these enamels, a school of painters was already at work in Bilston in connection with the japan trade, which is known to have been established immediately after the accession of George I. Techniques of japanning and enamelling differed, but an intelligent painter would soon become accomplished in either medium. Box-painting became a recognized trade. In 1755 Hannah Taylor was apprenticed to Thomas Bayliss, a box painter of Bilston. The *Directory* of 1770 mentions only John Perry as an enamel painter, probably because he was the most important, employing others to copy from his patterns while he supervised the firing processes. George Stubbs, R. A., was at one time an enameller in Perry's workshops.

No specific work can be assigned to any one artist, although individual hands may be recognized. Decoration copying was a monotonous job and most of the repetitive work was done by girls.

John Vardon (*d.* 1792), entered in the 1770 *Directory* as 'engraver and painter', was another, more important, master decorator. The term 'engraver' must be interpreted in its contemporary local sense as meaning an engraver or printer of transfer designs for enamels. To Vardon's workshops the smaller enamellers sent their enamel blanks for decoration in transfer-printing and over-painting. Son of the rector of Darlaston, he was established in Bilston as early as March 1756, when the parish register recorded the baptism of his child. Whether Vardon actually engraved his own copper-plates is uncertain; until 1770 he may have bought originals from Robert Hancock. Certainly it is unlikely that he held a local monopoly.

In any case, Hancock, with his Battersea experience, and perhaps even his own toy-making business in Birmingham, must assuredly have been well known to the trade generally. His engraving shops are proved to have supplied transfer designs to Worcester, and a number of enamellers as yet unidentified. Eventually, no doubt, it will be proved that he supplied ready-printed paper transfers to the trade. After leaving Worcester in 1774, where for a short time he had been a partner in the porcelain works, he is found at Tividale and at Oldbury, both in the Bilston–Wednesbury area. Some transfer-prints were exceptionally well produced and these might be his work. The print, signed R.H.*f.*, of 'The Tea Party', of which variants appear on Bow and Worcester porcelain, figures on an enamel box set in a scroll-surrounded reserve (Plate 44) in the Ionides collection. Such treatment, on a coloured box with raised diaper decoration, immediately suggests Bilston of the best period rather than Battersea work.

Enamellers in a large way, such as the Beckett and Perry families, might employ their own engravers, however, to prepare copper-plates for transfer work. The output of enamels from Bilston must have been colossal, transfer work becoming particularly prominent from about 1780. Unfortunately, the majority of these prints were taken from crudely engraved copper-plates and as crudely washed with colour. The small, unimportant snuff-boxes and patch-boxes, of which hundreds of thousands were produced in South Staffordshire and Birmingham, bear no evidence of a master hand. Rather are they indicative of a new and cheaper technique evolved to suit the demands of mass-production pricing. Today, these amusing enamel 'trifles' have their own niche among collectors' items, but they must not be allowed to obscure the more considerable claims of Bilston enamels.

Regarding the enamellers of Birmingham, the established facts are scanty indeed. Reference has been made already to the early work of John Taylor and the considerable facilities for the design and practice of industrial art reported by him in 1759. By 1770, Matthew Boulton of the Soho, Birmingham, firm of Boulton and Fothergill, was in a position to report on the manufacture of enamels to James Adam the architect, brother of the more famous Robert Adam, in a letter dated August 14, 1770, adding, 'I have seven or eight hundred persons employed in almost all those Arts that are applicable to the manufacturing of all the metals, the simi metals and various combinations of them, also Tortois shell, Enamels, &c. &c.' Already, at that date, Boulton was engaged in the manufacture of Sheffield plate: in 1768 Dr Darwin noted this in full production. Since no other manufacturer outside Sheffield was making plated ware until after 1770, the Boulton and Fothergill firm was in an unrivalled position to produce the large and elaborate enamelled pieces now so rare and valuable. No other enamellers would have possessed tools which could shape the more complex copper bodies.

At the same time, the enamelling furnaces were improved during the 1770's so that these large pieces could be fired without danger of subsequent flaking of the enamel. There is reason to think that the Soho firm was the source of the most ambitious pieces of decorative enamel ever produced. Some enamelled candlesticks are exact reproductions in size and shape of some plated candlesticks stamped with the so-called sun—really the Garter star—of Matthew Boulton. Moreover, candlesticks such as a pair in the Ionides collection, made with enamelled bodies in the spirally fluted square-based style, were sometimes topped with Sheffield plate sconces. In some instances it might be argued that such loose sconces were later replacements, but in the Ionides examples the note of silver is repeated in the silver-lustred bosses decorating their bases. Such silver lustre was achieved not with silver but with platinum and was an innovation on pottery in the 1790's, made possible by technical developments dating from 1784. Its introduction in conjunction with Sheffield plate on handsome candlesticks of a particularly pleasant turquoise blue was precisely the kind of experiment that might be expected of Matthew Boulton.

Another experiment which may be credited to this pioneer concerns the association of tortoiseshell with enamelled toys. In about 1780 Boulton acquired the tortoiseshell business of John Gimblett, another enthusiast for industrialization who, as early as 1765, had established the first factory for producing watches in quantity, at Snow Hill, Birmingham. The rare tortoiseshell-lined enamel snuff-box may well be an experimental outcome of Boulton's action, the shell obviously being an improvement for containing the snuff. From another specimen in the Ionides collection it would appear that experiments were also made in applying the shell to the outside of an enamel box, decorated with laborious piqué work, but the shell did not adhere easily to the smooth enamel surface. Occasional boxes are found made of tortoiseshell with painted enamel lids.

In many respects the firm of Boulton and Fothergill was exceptional, both in its development of new and 'foreign' ideas and practices and in the quality of workmanship maintained. The firm was responsible for some of the finest ormolu work ever produced in England. Elaborately designed mounts made from the pinchbeck group of alloys (see Chapter Nine) would come naturally to its high-class designers and craftsmen. In addition to large pieces such as candlesticks and caskets, therefore, the firm may well be credited with many of the most exquisitely finished and mounted enamels that remain a particular joy to the collector. Among these may be mentioned the elaborately fitted étuis, such as those with delicately hand-tooled mounts decorated with tiny flowers and leaves or formal patterns in low relief (Plates 33 and 34). Such workmanship is matched by the contents of these pieces, variously designed to meet personal needs for the toilet, for embroidery work, drawing, and so on. Of brilliant gilt-metal, each fitting into an appropriate slot in a metal and wood framework, these might include scissors, pencil, rule, bodkin, a tiny spoon, a two-pronged fork which, with accompanying steel knife blade, fitted into hollow handles, and a slip of ivory for memoranda. Such pieces could not have been more carefully finished if made of gold. An example in the collection of Her Majesty Queen Mary has the maker's initials *B & F* stamped on the gilt-metal spoon. So far as the authors are aware this is the only manufacturer's mark yet identified stamped on equipment directly connected with an enamel. A very few pieces such as étuis have silver mounts, but the hall-marks are rarely complete. Sometimes a sovereign's head duty-mark is decipherable, dating the piece to 1784 or later. Unfortunately, knife blades made in Birmingham, unlike Sheffield work, carried no cutlers' marks.

Equally delightful as typifying painted enamel-work at its best are the tiny writing-sets (Plate 36). These, usually measuring only $2\frac{3}{4} \times 2\frac{3}{8} \times 1\frac{1}{2}$ inches, were fitted with gilt-metal pen and nibs, a glass fob-seal, and minute ink and pounce bottles of faceted glass with decorated enamel tops. In the Ionides collection is a pair of steel snuffers of notable quality, decorated with small medallions of painted enamel.

In 1776 Matthew Boulton sent a representative to St Petersburg to introduce the art manufactures for which he was already famous and to take orders, hoping 'to supplant the French as well in plate as in gilt'. The Empress Catherine found Boulton's productions superior in every way to those of France and bought a wide variety of goods. Members of the Court followed the royal example. From time to time, fine English enamels have been brought from Russia and these must necessarily have been made in Boulton's Soho factory. Occasional examples even display some attempt to incorporate Russian words in the decoration, but not in a manner intelligible to a Russian.

Information regarding other Birmingham enamellers is still very imperfect. Many may well have restricted themselves to minor pieces. For instance, Basil Palmer is entered in the 1767 *Directory* as an enameller and button-maker, but nothing further has been recorded concerning him. Among those who continued the craft well into the nineteenth century may be mentioned: J. Abrahall, 4 Caroline Street; John Brown and Company, 69 Bull Street; Charles Gwynne, 16 Mott Street; Perton and Subin, 82 Caroline Street. These were recorded as late as 1839 in *Robson's Directory*.

Enamelling at Wednesbury began within a few months of the Bickley sale at Bilston in 1776. It was probably from this source that Samuel Yardley, first of the Wednesbury enamellers, obtained the necessary equipment. The men associated with the manufacture of enamels in this town included three generations of Yardleys, and the families of Holden, Ross, Baker, and Snape. All became rich. The Holden family, for instance, lived in Lower High Street, Wednesbury, and enjoyed 'at the rear of their house a garden adorned with statues, fountains and stone-seated alcoves'.

The trade *Directory* for 1783 gives the names of several manufacturers under the title of 'Enamellers in General', indicating a well-established industry, and there are several nineteenth-century references to the quality of the work. G. A. Cooke, writing in the *Complete Itinerary of the County of Stafford*, published in 1801, recorded that at Wednesbury 'Enamel paintings are done here in the highest perfection and beauty'. In 1813 Nightingale's *Beauties of England and Wales* stated that 'enamel painting in the finest style of execution are among Wednesbury's more prominent productions'. Pitt's *History of Staffordshire*, published in 1817, said that 'the finest enamel paintings are among the productions of Wednesbury's artists'.

Samuel Yardley I is considered by some to have been responsible for introducing to the enamel trade new methods of producing mounts with the aid of machinery, and for developing a certain flamboyancy of colour and pattern. His son, Samuel II, was chiefly occupied in nursing the business through the early years of the Napoleonic wars. Yardley enamels are known to have been highly glossy and the basic enamel dead white. The Yardleys overcame the war-time depression and John Yardley (1770–1854) was entered in the *Directory* of 1817 as an 'enamel box and toy watch maker'. These toy watches were merely hollow shams, with hands and hours painted on their dials. They had a great vogue with the miners and ironworkers of the Black Country, who wore them with their Sunday best, attached to great rattling chains of tinned wire. Similar watches, nearly a foot in diameter, hung in the bars of public-houses.

Appropriately enough, John Yardley, of Church Hill, grandson of the founder of the Wednesbury enamel trade, was one of the last of the South Staffordshire enamellers. He abandoned the business in 1840.

At the dispersal of John Yardley's effects in 1859, several clothes-baskets full of enamels were sold to a dealer at a few shillings for each basket. These contained, among other things, boxes, buttons, studs and links, plaques, medallions and small trays in perfect condition. F. W. Hackwood, in *Wednesbury Workshops*, says that the Yardley firm also made patch-boxes, snuffboxes, tea-caddies, salt-cellars, brooches, and breast-pins for frilled shirt-fronts, door-knobs and finger-plates.

Hackwood, writing in the *Wednesbury Borough News*, April 11, 1925, recollects that his earliest employment consisted of breaking up small unwanted and superfluous stock, to recover the copper frames and discs for sale as scrap. Late in life Hackwood formed a collection of Wednesbury enamels, now in the Wednesbury Art Gallery. Mr Whitaker, a former editor of the Wolverhampton *Express and Star*, has recorded that in the Bilston–Wednesbury area 'unfinished ovals from the tops of small boxes were common during the 1860's as card counters'.

Little is known concerning other Wednesbury enamellers. James Ross (1745–1821), an apprentice of Robert Hancock's from 1765 until Hancock went to Worcester, made a fortune by specializing in pink enamels. No doubt

Ross learned the technicalities of enamelling from Hancock, afterwards becoming well known as an engraver of copper-plates for transfer-printing on pottery and porcelain in a style reminiscent of his master. Like Hancock, Ross sometimes signed copper-plates with a partly hidden signature, often so small that it might be invisible without the aid of a magnifying glass.

Local writers occasionally refer to Ross's pink enamels, but fail to record the date of his establishment in Wednesbury. It was not earlier than 1783, however, nor later than 1785, at a time when Hancock was living in the district and possibly assisted in an advisory capacity. Hackwood's *Wednesbury Workshops* refers briefly to Ross:

> It has been handed down in connection with one of these [Wednesbury] enamellers named James Ross, that this gentleman discovered the secret of a pigment which gave to some of their best wares a delicate pink tint, so greatly admired by purchasers that in a short space he amassed a fortune. This shade of pink was the envy of all other manufacturers, but the secret of its production was well kept, until at last it was obtained from Mrs Ross in the hunting field by means of the most unscrupulous that can be conceived.

Few Wednesbury decorators are known and none of their work is distinguishable. Moses Haughton (1734–1804) of Wednesbury is referred to in Bryan's *Dictionary of Painters* as 'being brought up as an enamel painter under a Mr Holden' and 'afterwards went to Birmingham where he was employed in the manufactories there as an ornamenter of tea-boards'. This is highly improbable, for the Holdens were not established in Wednesbury as enamellers until about 1780, when Haughton was about forty-six years old. His monument in St Philip's Cathedral Church, Birmingham, states that he was for more than forty years a resident of Birmingham. He must have left Wednesbury, then, in about 1764. This was the period referred to in the Wednesbury Art Gallery Catalogue (1930) which says:

> When Henry Clay and Baskerville [the famous Birmingham japanners] essayed to raise the manufacture of japanned tea trays and similar articles to the rank of a fine art, they sent for Moses Haughton to do the hand painting for them, and for many years the artist appears to have worked at the factory they had established in Birmingham.

The more likely theory is that he had been employed as a decorator in his younger days by William Holden (1690–1780), a master japanner and Haughton's uncle by marriage. In 1805 Holden's great-grandson married the daughter of Henry Clay. The possibility is therefore very remote that Moses Haughton was at any time a decorator of enamels at Wednesbury.

Wednesbury Art Gallery possesses a small collection of enamels said to be the work of Thomas Wilkes, of whom a miniature portrait is exhibited. Although acquired by purchase from Wilkes's great-granddaughter, some of the enamels suggest manufacture at a date later than the death of Thomas Wilkes in 1782. The church register, recording his death, described him as a painter. Another entry in the same register tells us that John Wright, painter, was buried in 1783.

Lewis Hackwood, born at Wednesbury in 1766, was apprenticed as an engraver to James Ross. During the depression following the French Revolution, he found his place as an engraver to the pottery trade and eventually became one of Wedgwood's finest engravers. A master copper-plate engraver and painter of Wednesbury enamels was John Harper. Decorations from his own hand were usually dead-game pieces. His canvas paintings are now being collected.

The enamel factories of Wednesbury were commodious premises. Hackwood refers to them as three-story buildings and well lighted, specifying one in Meeting Street and another at the corner of High Bullen and Upper High Street, but omitting to give the names of the enamellers who occupied them.

Chapter Six

MANUFACTURING PROCESSES

So many varieties of colourful trinkets are widely and inexpensively available today that it may be difficult to appreciate how much the eighteenth-century enamellers accomplished, how many obstacles they overcame, and how many details in their products may have been dictated not by choice but by the limitations of currently available materials and methods. The simplest little enamel snuff-box involved a series of specialist processes, for which accepted practices had to be modified, or entirely new ones devised. It was only by slow degrees that the decorators obtained complete mastery over colour, for instance, and could tell with accuracy what shades their designs would have acquired by the time they emerged from the firing ovens. And the whole range of firing work itself involved endless difficulties of heat adjustment and even distribution: a variety of problems had to be eliminated before pieces of any considerable size could be fired.

By a painted enamel, whether it be a button or a casket, is implied an article made of metal, usually copper, and coated with enamel—a vitreous substance of glass toughened with lead oxide, made opaque white by the addition of oxide of tin or arsenic, and sometimes stained with colour—and decorated with lines or washes of fusible pigment applied by brush or transfer. What these eighteenth-century enamellers produced, therefore, was really tough, opaque glass surrounding a central core of metal, to which it was attached by fusion caused by its subjection to intense heat. Provided only that the enamel could be made to adhere to the thin central sheet of copper, so that changes of atmosphere and temperature left it unaffected, it proved a material which would stand up to long years of ordinary use with no deterioration whatever of its decorative qualities.

At first its use in England was confined to small plaques, oval or rectangular, and to simple boxes and the like constructed of fairly similarly shaped pieces held together by metal mounts. But before the end of the eighteenth century it was mainly the question of the cost of materials and labour in relation to demand for the finished product that imposed limits upon the decorative pieces the enameller produced in this amenable material. In the Ionides collection is a magnificent set of knives and forks with matching enamelled handles, enclosed in an enamelled knife-box which has the sloping lid and serpentine shaping of the late eighteenth century.

Whatever the object being made, the same basic work was involved. The central core of paper-thin copper had to be cut out and jointed, pressed, or hammered into the required shape. This was then entirely coated on both sides with layers of white enamel, affixed by firing. This smooth surface was then variously decorated, subjected to further firings, and, finally, fitted into simple or elaborate mounts.

In attempting to see the work all this involved for enamellers of the mid-eighteenth century it is useful to consult contemporary craft books, among which none is more revealing than *The Handmaid to the Arts*. While it is generally recognized that this two-volume work may well have had considerable effect in encouraging the trade during the years immediately following its publication—years that witnessed the general development of English painted enamels—it has not been so generally appreciated, perhaps, that Robert Dossie's book came close on the heels of the immensely larger French work, *Encyclopédie ou dictionnaire raisonné des sciences, des arts et des métiers*, published in Paris in 1755. It would be interesting to know how much eighteenth century enamellers owed directly or indirectly to Diderot's monumental encyclopaedia.

The first requirement of the enameller was the thin sheet of copper forming the core to which the enamel was fused. According to Robert Dossie, these copper-plates were 'beaten to a proper thickness and then passed betwixt a pair of very fine steel rollers very closely set, and drawn as thin as possible to retain a proper tenacity'. When the metal reached paper-thickness— 0.01 of an inch being usual—it was hammered, stamped, or jointed so as to form the shape required. Blanks were cut from the rolled sheet-copper with a mallet and a steel punch of the required shape. Steel punches used for cutting blanks for hollow-ware of intricate shape, such as boxes in the form of birds' heads, were made in sections.

The most obvious method of shaping boxes and the like was by joining pieces of the flat metal at the corners. So thin was the copper sheet that a flat lap-joint was indiscernible when covered on both sides with coatings of enamel. Instead of lap-jointing, some enamellers tied each corner of their boxes with a slender copper ribbon drawn through two holes pierced in the sides. In building a large piece, such as an oval tea-caddy, the parts were joined by a hammered overlap known as the Roman joint.

Those blanks which required rounding out were placed upon a slightly concave 'anvil' of hard wood and struck with a hard-wood mallet having a convex face of similar shape. This shaping was done without impairing the smoothness of the metal surface. Such methods of handling copper blanks were used throughout the history of English enamelling.

The invention of stamping in 1769 by Richard Ford, a Birmingham maker of gilt 'toys', enabled large, shapely hollow-ware to be produced more speedily. So thin was the copper generally used by enamellers that the stamp could only be applied to a limited extent, and hand-raising was never superseded. Nevertheless, some large pieces were raised with the aid of this machine, the copper blank being of a thicker gauge for this purpose. The blank was placed upon a die or raised model of the pattern desired, and a hammer containing a similar model of concave shape, moving between two vertical rods, was allowed to fall upon it, thus forming the metal as required. Until the introduction of a long-wearing cast steel during the 1790's, only smooth-surfaced, shallow objects were stamped. Candlestick bases were struck to a smooth shape approximating to the required design and finished by hand-raising. Cast steel made economically possible the cutting of more intricate dies and was directly responsible for a new and cheaper series of animal-head boxes.

The rims of ink standishes, card-counter trays, and similar pieces were decorated with perforations by means of hand-punches of various shapes, again made from the new cast steel. Such perforated rims were but one of the many ways in which enamellers sought to produce inexpensive approximations of recent porcelain fashions. It will be noted that such pieces show various characteristics of very late eighteenth-century workmanship, being dipped in conspicuously thin enamel and lacking all raised decoration.

Suitably shaped, the copper was annealed to make it hold its form, a process which also cleaned grease, oil, and other impurities from its surface.

After cooling, it was plunged into dilute nitric acid for four minutes, then rinsed thoroughly in cold water. The copper-bright surfaces were then roughened with a harsh brush of brass wires and they were ready for the first application of the enamel.

The problem of thermal expansion was overcome by applying the enamel thickly and evenly on both sides of the copper, which was usually given a slight but definite curve to reduce the risk of unsightly warping. The metal was thus held expanded between two layers of enamel, successive firings actually increasing the size of a piece. The copper was merely a fragile skeleton supporting enamel many times thicker than itself. After firing, the article was, in effect, a piece of opaque white reinforced glass which could be coloured, gilded, or printed upon like porcelain but was immensely stronger.

The enamels themselves were prepared from rule-of-thumb formulae and their ingredients were seldom of uniform quality owing to the presence of impurities. The only test the sifted materials were given was the 'thumb-nail' test. The dark specks often found embedded in the white ground surface of fired enamels are due chiefly to impurities. Small bubbles in the enamel surface indicate that firing was insufficiently prolonged.

This firing was carried out in furnaces known to the enamellers as muffles because oxidization was reduced by muffling or damping the draught. The muffles were of wrought iron and each was only large enough to contain one clay case or 'coffin' in which the enamel-coated articles were placed for the burning or fusing process. Pit-coal was used for firing these furnaces, as in the enamelling districts it was considerably cheaper than charcoal and the coffins could be sealed securely from the fumes and smoke. A peep-hole was provided in the door of each muffle through which the enameller could see how a test piece of enamel was faring. To safeguard his eyes from the intense heat, he covered his head with a loose helmet of cloth fitted at eye-level with a rectangle of tinted glass. Working at night with strangely muffled faces in flickering red firelight, these enamellers created the legend in Bilston that they were fiends in league with the devil.

The purpose of the coffin, which was made of Stourbridge clay or tobacco-pipe clay, was to protect the enamels from injury by smoke or fumes from the fire while being burned. It measured ten inches by six inches by seven inches deep. The corners were fitted with three-inch columns to support a wrought-iron tray containing a second layer of enamel-work. The coffins were thickly chalked inside to prevent the contents from sticking. An iron instrument resembling a three-foot-long baker's peel was used for lifting the coffins into and out of the furnace.

Suitably coated with enamel, the objects to be fired were laid in the coffin and its lid sealed at the joints with plastic fire-lute. To test the furnace, a piece of tile coated with enamel of the same quality as that used on the objects within the coffin was laid on the lid. The coffin was first warmed on the dome of the furnace to prevent cracking, then placed within it, well away from the sides. Particular care had to be taken when inserting the coffin to ensure that the contents were not shaken so as to loosen the enamel or cause it to fall away from the copper sheets. Inside the coffin the copper and the pulverized enamel with which it was coated became bright white in the intense heat.

When firing was completed the coffin was removed and again placed on the furnace top so that cooling would be gradual and the enamel toughened. If the cooling was too rapid the enamel was liable later to crack or scale off.

Individual pieces of enamel were limited in size by the small capacity of the muffles. For this reason candlesticks were made in sections, the foot and sconce rims and the joints in the stem being mounted alike with double-gilt metal. Small taper-sticks were sometimes enamelled in single pieces, but the tall, classical stem candlesticks could only be made after about 1780, when muffle length had been increased. Even as late as 1851 the Jury's Report on enamels at the Great Exhibition recorded the impossibility of making any enamel more than twelve inches square except by the joining of segments after enamelling.

Dossie gives many interesting details regarding the composition of the enamels which had to undergo this process, stressing that 'if the painting is to be in the nature of a picture or demand a variety of colours, a ground colour of white must be laid on the metal. This hard ground body must necessarily be of the same vitreous nature as the softer flux [the body in which the colours were mixed to bind them to the ground] which melted at a lower temperature than the ground colour.' Obviously, if both melted at the same temperature they would merge into a single homogeneous coating. No other substance is capable of enduring such a great heat and at the same time possesses the property of binding itself firmly to the copper surface. When several colours were superimposed they were made to consist of materials which melted at progressively lower firing temperatures.

The Handmaid to the Arts quotes five recipes for the preparation of white ground enamels, of which three appear suitable for taking colours. One of these instructs the enameller:

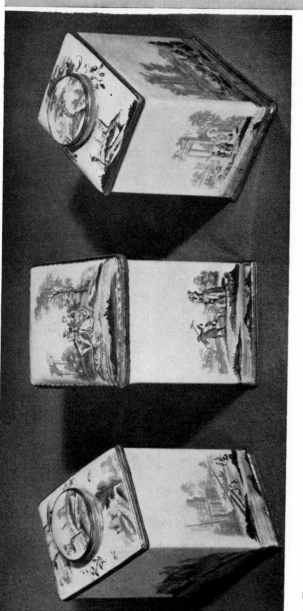

57. Two tea-canisters and a sugar-box of flawless white enamel showing particularly effective use of monochrome purple transfer-printing strengthened and emphasized by the hand painting of foreground details in a deeper tone of the same colour. Like many good quality boxes, the sugar-box has the inner edges of the rim mount tooled in serrated outlines. It may be noted that the enameller had so perfectly mastered his technique in these boxes that he required neither metal mounts nor raised enamel decoration to mask the sharp angles of the sides. In each instance, however, the base as well as the shoulders were given the protection of a metal mount, a detail which was omitted from many a later box.

58. A large bodkin holder, 5¼ inches long and 1 inch in diameter. The ground colour is a beautiful medium blue, with small white diaper patterns and gilt scrolls, stars and other detached *motifs*. There are four white reserves, each painted in considerable detail with a pastoral or harbour scene. The metal work is restricted to the rims of the opening, the ends of the little cylinder being neatly rounded and finished with stars of raised enamel-work. Typically, this bodkin holder closes without any fastening, the perfection of the fit making it secure.

59. *Above: La Belle Aventure* by François Boucher, engraved by P. Aveline, was one of the several fortune-teller subjects popular with eighteenth-century enamel decorators. This particularly handsome rendering, measuring $8 \times 6\frac{1}{4}$ inches, is a careful piece of hand painting. *Below:* Considerable success was achieved with purely pictorial landscape work in enamels, such as this well-designed scene in the popular Italian manner.

60. Interesting as an example of the composite decorative work found in a single box measuring no more than $3 \times 3\frac{1}{4} \times 1\frac{1}{2}$ inches. The lid shows an indifferent rendering of 'The Death of Leander' after Feti, but an inner lid carries a portrait showing a more competent hand. The rich colouring of the dress is set against a deep greyish olive-green background. The concave sides of the box suggest the work of yet another artist, with flowers and insects charmingly portrayed on exceptionally white enamel, and more flowers decorate the base.

61. Left: A box decorated with a spirited painting of the famous racehorse Gimcrack, foaled in 1760. Right: A fortune-telling scene. The same subject appears on a red-printed plaque attributed to Battersea, No. 50 in the Schreiber collection, Victoria and Albert Museum.

62. A well-painted box, the lid subject being a free adaptation of Lancret's 'Autumn' from the engraving by J. Simon.

63. Notably clear, strong black transfer-prints, hand-coloured, on a base of high quality, decorate this deep pink box which measures $3\frac{1}{4} \times 2\frac{1}{8} \times 1\frac{1}{4}$ inches.

64. Four scent bottles showing their particular suitability to the enameller's technique. Each is painted on front and back, as was customary in all such work, which was intended to be viewed from any angle. *Extreme left:* An exceptionally elaborate little bottle of an unusual shape. In addition to the normal gilt-metal stopper and rim, this has a metal-mounted base, hinged as a tiny patch-box and with a painted enamel 'lid'. This may be compared with the typical bonbonnière in bird or animal form which stands on a hinged painted enamel lid. *Left, centre:* The most typical bottle design, but with a dolphin instead of the usual bird stopper. The figure painting is in a style popular on high quality bottles, representing 'Taste' from Houston's series of 'Senses'. *Right, centre:* A pyriform bottle in the footed outline popular at this period in silverware. *Extreme right:* A rich little bottle, the painting of fruit against a dark background being in the meticulous, three-dimensional style associated with particularly well-mounted étuis and boxes.

116

65. Six scent bottles, the tallest 4 inches high, indicating the range of decorative treatment lavished on these essential small *galanteries* of the period: *Above, left:* Deep pink, the two reserves hand painted with water scenes in bright colours. *Centre:* Pale yellow and pale green background press-embossed to emphasize the elaborate gilded scrolls surrounding the flat picture reserves. These show the fishing scene and the man with dog and gun illustrated in *The Ladies Amusement*. *Right:* White, with soft turquoise green and mauve bosses and pale yellow and mauve lines down the neck, and patterned in raised white and gilt. Press-shaped and with painted reserves showing a man and woman walking, and a man fishing. *Below, left:* White, in an unusual shape, colourfully painted with lively birds and scattered flower posies. *Centre:* Another example in which the two sides of the metal core of the bottle were press-embossed before being joined together. The bottle is quickly decorated with stripes of various colours, and gilded scrolls, but shows a carefully painted head of a woman holding a mask from Houston's popular engraving of Philippe Mercier's 'Night'. *Right:* Yet another treatment, the body pale yellow gilt over the slight embossing suggestive of basket-work. The flower decoration is repeated in the gilt-metal stopper, less usual than the bird silhouette.

117

66. Four views of a unique little box shaped as a globe, its diameter $1\frac{7}{8}$ inches. Europe and America occupy one hemisphere, Asia and Africa the other, with the metal-rimmed opening, neatly hinged and fitted with twisted wire lifter, serving as equator. The white ground enamel is notably good. The paintings are in colour, and purple-flowered scrolls surround the names which are in black.

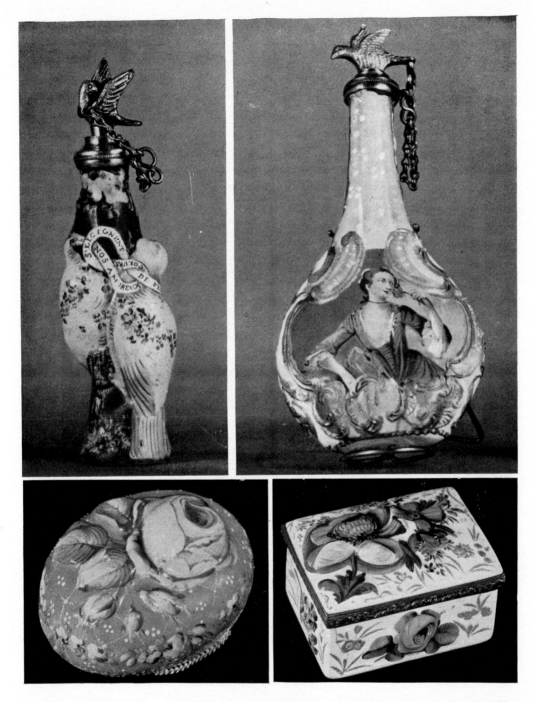

67. *Above:* Scent bottles were among the most elaborately fashioned little enamels of their period. That on the left is in the shape of two doves, their beaks holding a scroll with a love-knot bearing a somewhat faulty French inscription. The specimen on the right is more conventional.

68. *Below:* Two examples of press-embossed boxes. *Left:* The lid is deeply domed and the box portion comparatively shallow. *Right:* A box having a creamy white background to the highly embossed flowers.

69. In pursuit of further novelties, enamellers made boxes and bottles in many human and animal forms. The bottle on the left is a 3-inch representation of Flora Macdonald, taken from Richard Wilson's portrait. In addition to the neck opening there is a shallow box in the base. The face is painted in natural colours, the plaid blue and yellow, and there are flowers in full colour on the slightly convex base. The head to the right is 2¾ inches high: the back, painted to resemble cap and hair, opens so that the article can be used as a box.

70. Typical of the small plaques and box lids of the late eighteenth-century enameller, these little pieces, measuring 2⅛ and 2⅞ inches at their greatest diameters, are transfer-printed in sepia on white grounds.

Take of flint-glass one pound, of calx of tin or putty of the first degree of whiteness half a pound, of pearl-ashes and common salt each four ounces, and of borax one ounce. The ingredients being thoroughly mixt by grinding them together on a porphyry stone, or by pounding and rubbing them well in a glass mortar, put them into a proper melting pot, and give them a moderate heat till they incorporate thoroughly; but the fusion should not be either strong or long continued; for, if the glass be perfectly liquefied, the calx of tin is apt to subside; and, consequently, to be unequally mixt in the mass when cold. When the heat has had its due effect, take the pot out of the fire and pour the matter on a clean iron plate, or into moulders to form it into cakes.

This enamel, if the calx of tin be perfectly good, will be very white ... it will also bear colours very well, where such a ground is wanted for any painting; but if it be found too soft, in proportion to the fluxes of the colours, it may be prepared of a greater degree of hardness by omitting the borax.

Oxide of tin was an ingredient of the finest enamels. Flint-glass merely opacified with arsenic was used for the cheaper, later work. Examples have been seen where the copper has apparently been enclosed within a very thick covering of greenish flux which, in its turn, has been covered with a film of opaque enamel and then decorated. This translucent flux was brittle and did not adhere well to the copper. Few examples have survived in good condition.

The white enamel, as prepared or bought from a glasshouse, was crushed in a hardened steel mill until reduced to a sand-like powder. This was washed in clear water and, the heavier ingredients having subsided, the remaining milky-looking liquid was drawn off and left to settle in a separate vessel. This process was repeated until three qualities of powder were secured and placed in glass vessels. Each quality of powder was covered with nitric acid for twelve hours and occasionally stirred with a glass spatula in order to dissolve any metallic particles abraded from the steel mortar. These would impair the whiteness of the fired enamel if not removed. When the acid had been poured off, the enamel was washed in several waters until completely acid-free. The powder was then covered with clean water until required for use.

The early enamels received their ground coating of costly white enamel from brush or spatula. The finely ground enamel was sifted through a hair sieve and mixed with oil of lavender. The time between its application and firing was brief because the binding oil quickly evaporated, allowing the enamel to crumble away as powder. A less expensive method was sometimes used by the early Bilston enamellers. The copper surface was given a film of oil of lavender and finely powdered enamel was spread over this until the proper thickness was reached. The oil of lavender might be diluted with turpentine, but this tended to leave the finished surface sprinkled with dark spots. Consequently the use of this cheaper method was most frequently restricted to the interiors of cheap boxes and the backs of plaques.

With the invention of a less expensive enamelling process by which the copper was dipped into liquid enamel, it became usual to apply a second and even a third coating of base enamel, the outer covering consisting of an enamel film of very fine texture.

The liquid enamel was prepared in small portable dipping tanks, the test for correct consistency being to dip the hand in the enamel and watch it run from the finger tips. Water was added until it looked right, about one and a half ounces of enamel being required to cover about one square foot of copper.

The working enamellers themselves were seldom familiar with the formulae used, these being the personal property of master enamellers, who seldom divulged their secrets. Nathaniel Hadley, the last recorded employee in the Wednesbury enamel trade, has placed on record that flint-glass in the form of broken public-house goblets was an ingredient to which he saw added 'sea sand, red lead and arsenic'. These were melted together in a crucible and after solidifying were crushed to a fine powder in the mill. This was the basis of white enamel to which a colour might be added for a final coating if a tinted background were needed. The presence of arsenic introduced an element of danger to the health of the operators concerned. The only protection taken was by the mixers, who tied handkerchiefs over their mouths and nostrils.

The actual enamelling was usually done by a woman seated at a stool next to a drying stove and having before her a vessel containing liquid enamel resembling thick cream. The consistency of this liquid enamel was a matter of prime importance: frequently the liquid required diluting with additional water.

The worker would lift a shaped piece of copper, holding its edges between finger and thumb so as not to touch any part where perfection of surface was essential. Holding it thus in her left hand over the tank of enamel, she spooned or ladled the liquid over its upper surface. Then, putting down the ladle, she used her free hand to give two or three smart taps to the hand still holding the enamel. This shook superfluous enamel from the copper, simultaneously distributing the thin coating more evenly over the metal surface. Much of the quality of the finished enamel depended upon the neatness with which this operation was performed. Evenly spread and well-packed enamel meant an avoidance of hollows below the surface after melting and ensured a high degree of smoothness. The blank was then placed upon a stove to dry. Next, liquid enamel was ladled over the inner surface and drained, a similar smart tap was given to distribute the enamel evenly, and the piece was dried as before.

The blank, coated with dry powdered enamel on both sides, was then fired in the furnace. After completion of the first firing, the enamel was cleaned with a very weak solution of nitric acid. The second layer of enamel, made from the finer settlings, was then applied and fired. Afterwards a thin layer of the finest and whitest portion of the enamel was applied, to the exterior surface only, and the piece was fired yet again.

Cheap enamels lacked the gloss which appeared naturally on those of good quality. Such pieces were therefore glazed over the decoration, whether this was painted or transfer-printed. A single coating of glaze was applied in a similar manner to the layers which built up the enamel. As the glaze was required to be transparent it consisted entirely of powdered flint-glass. This was washed, ground in a mill, then finely sieved. Again, it was even more thoroughly ground until reduced to the finest powder possible. This was mixed with water to a consistency thinner than that of the enamel, applied to the decorated object in a similar manner, and given a final firing in the muffle.

Reference has already been made to Nathaniel Hadley of Oakeswell End, near Wednesbury, who died in 1895. Hadley had been continuously employed in the Wednesbury enamel trade throughout the period of its decline. F. W. Hackwood, in search of material for his book, *Wednesbury Workshops*, published in 1889, interviewed Hadley and obtained a first-hand description of the methods used by John Yardley of Wednesbury, the last of the old English master enamellers. The processes used were more or less traditional and common throughout the trade.

The primitive equipment used during the declining years was largely identical with that of eighty years earlier. It is notable that some speeding-up processes accepted by the general toy trade during the 1780's were never utilized by the enamellers. Employees were chiefly women and children, whose hours were from 6 A.M. to 8 P.M. six days a week, the children being expected to put in an extra half-day's work on Sunday for cleaning the equipment.

Chapter Seven

DECORATION: HAND PAINTING, TRANSFER-PRINTING, GILDING

IT has been noted that the colours appearing on known products of the Battersea factory tended to be simple and limited in range, suggesting incomplete mastery of the colouring technique. On the other hand, the white basis to the enamels was extremely fine. At this period the best quality of enamel was imported from Murano under the name of 'Venetian white hard enamel' and was composed of silica, borax, and oxide of tin. It is scarcely surprising, therefore, to find in 1765, when painted enamels were coming to the fore in South Staffordshire and Birmingham, that the Society of Arts set about attempting to improve home production of the raw materials. In that year the Society offered two prizes for improved enamels, each to the value of £50. One was offered to any person in England or Wales 'who shall make the best white enamel, the same being equal in colour, and all other properties to the Venetian'.

The other prize of £50 was offered to 'the person who shall make the finest true Red colour for the use of Enamel painters, which shall bear repeated and sufficiently strong fires without change; the quantity to be produced not less than two ounces, from which a quarter of an ounce will be taken for trials. Preference will be given to that colour which approaches nearest to fine vermilion. No regard will be had to any that verges at all toward the purple.'

The fact that such considerable prizes were offered indicates that even in contemporary eyes the enamels generally available did not appear wholly satisfactory, and that those who sought to foster the painted enamel trade appreciated the detrimental effect of inferior materials. Coloured enamels were very expensive indeed. To such a degree of fineness was it necessary to reduce the powders that 'the labour of half a day was employed in grinding a drachm'—eight working days, probably well over a hundred hours, for the grinding of one ounce of coloured enamel.

By 1764, in the second edition of *The Handmaid to the Arts*, Dossie was able to list a considerable variety of colours and tones used by contemporary enamellers. These included scarlet or crimson-red, dark red, pink, rose-red, several shades of blue, yellow, brown, pink, light and dark green, orange, purple, red-brown, olive-brown, and black. As was customary with trade practices in the eighteenth century, the various ways of mixing and applying the coloured enamels were generally kept as personal 'secrets' by the master enamellers, some of whom died without leaving documentary instructions by which their business could be continued. Some at least of these old-time formulae were saved from oblivion, however, by 'an experienced professional person in the art of enamelling', Robert Wynn, of Wellington Place, Vauxhall, London. In 1817, Wynn communicated to the Society of Arts a dossier containing formulae for making coloured enamels such as had long been used for decorating the lids of good quality enamel boxes. The Society voted £20 to Wynn and placed specimens of the enamels in its repository.

Wynn warned his readers that previous published formulae had been compiled by writers unskilled in the craft. It was difficult to obtain a set of good enamel colours, and as a result the enamelling craft was regarded as something of a mystery. To counteract such a fallacy, he presented detailed instructions for the mixing of various reds, browns, blues, and so on, which are still on record in the Society's archives, together with Wynn's recipes for the transparent fluxes which were essential accompaniments of the colours.

A proportion of this more or less transparent flux was incorporated in each coloured enamel. The flux liquefied in the furnace more readily than the enamel and thus, when the decoration was fired, the flux in the white enamel base quickly united with that of the colour, and the colouring pigment was thereupon perfectly excluded from the air, surrounded by a dense vitrified mass. Wynn's recipes for fluxes consisted mainly of flint-glass and red lead, the aim being to introduce colourless calcined flints, sand, or other calcareous matter to ensure a resistant surface, which could not be obtained with the easily corroded salts, lead, arsenic, and similar flux ingredients.[1] Typical of Wynn's recipes was his flux No. 1: red lead, 8 parts by weight; borax calcined to a fine calx, $1\frac{1}{2}$ parts; flint powder, 2 parts; flint-glass, 6 parts. No. 2 flux consisted of: flint-glass, 10 parts by weight; white arsenic, 1 part; nitre, 1 part. For a very soft flux, to give a brilliant gloss to the enamel after firing, he recommended his No. 8: red lead, 6 parts by weight; borax not calcined, 4 parts; flint powder, 2 parts. After being melted the flux was poured on a wet flagstone, allowed to dry, then finely powdered.

In some of the finest enamel colours, too, Wynn recorded the introduction of powdered flint. In many of the cheaper products of South Staffordshire, however, it is evident that white sand—probably from Gornal—was used.

In this flint powder, flints, burnt white and cleaned with a brush and hot water, were made red-hot and then plunged into cold water. This was repeated several times and they were then ready to be pulverized in a mortar and finely ground in water.

With similar thoroughness Wynn described the preparation of such ingredients as red sulphate of iron. The sulphate of iron was pounded and placed in an earthenware muffle until all moisture evaporated, leaving a grey powder. This was placed in a crucible in a charcoal fire and stirred with a steel bar until it became red in colour. It was then poured into a pan of cold water and placed under a chimney which would disperse the fumes. When it had settled at the bottom of the pan it was washed several times in hot water and then dried for use. The more it was burnt, the darker red it became.

This was required as an ingredient of such colours as orange and light red. Thus orange consisted of: red lead, 12 parts; red sulphate of iron, 1 part; oxide of antimony, 4 parts; flint powder, 3 parts. These were mixed well, and calcined sufficiently to form a cohesive mass but without melting. One part of this mixture was combined with two and a half parts of a suitable flux and the whole ground for use. Only by such laborious processes did the enamellers achieve the lovely, durable colours which today appear as fresh as on the day they were applied.

Stressing the need to guard against the risk of blurring the design through placing the partly fired work in too hot a furnace, Wynn drew attention to

[1] The existence of the glass centre of Glassborough at Bilston, dating from the 1760's, where many of the enamel ingredients would be available, may have been one of the factors prompting the development of enamelling in this town.

the fact that the progressively softer enamel applied for the later, less intense, firings gave a rich, smooth surface to the finished work. When any hardening was required it was effected by adding more colouring matter to the enamel or by reducing the quantity of flux. If the colour needed softening, or if a brilliant shine was required after firing, a little more very soft flux might be added. Immediately it was prepared the coloured enamel was ground to a fine powder in water, dried before a fire, and stored in sealed bottles.

When required for painting, these powders were ground in spike oil of lavender or spirits of turpentine, and stiffened with thick oil of turpentine—a quality attained by the fluid oil of turpentine in three or four years. The finely powdered colours, tempered with the oil of lavender, were mixed on a china tile and applied with camel-hair or sable brushes, like any other paints. So volatile was the oil, however, that only small amounts of colour were mixed at a time. The oil was intended merely to convey the colour to the enamel, and was allowed to dry out by exposure to the air before firing. Even more important to the painter was the restriction which the firing process itself placed upon the work. Once it was fired, no error could be rectified except by grinding it out with crushed flint and an agate muller.

In comparison with the individual nature of enamel painting, the transfer-printing which might appear alone or as a basis for the painting was merely a routine process. Nevertheless, the work involved in the application of these transfer-prints had its own problems for the enameller. The potters, under the leadership of the first Josiah Spode, developed this method of decoration more fully, but even enamel-printing required considerable skill.

The basic process remained unchanged throughout the history of the enamel trade and was peculiar to English work. The design was incised with sharp steel tools on the surface of a flat copper-plate by the engraver, whose skill determined the quality of the finished work. Large numbers of impressions could be taken from each plate. The plate was warmed on a stove and then spread with special ink, which was rubbed well into the engraved lines with a broad, pliant knife, the surplus being cleaned off with a piece of beaver fur or flannel. The ink used for this purpose was known to the trade as printing-black—or brown, red, crimson, purple, mauve, brick-red—and was compounded to withstand the great heat which burnt it into the enamel. It was blended with special printer's oil, and the warmth of the copper-plate made the mixture sufficiently fluid to fill the most delicately engraved lines.

The inked copper-plate was next covered with a sheet of gummed paper, and plate and paper were wrapped in a double thickness of flannel. Wrapped in this way, they were subjected to considerable pressure, being passed several times between wooden rollers in a machine resembling a mangle and worked with a large wheel. In this way the inked design was drawn from the lines of the copper-plate and every finest detail made to adhere firmly to the paper.

With the flannel removed, the plate, still covered with the adhesive paper, was subjected to the heat of a drying stove. This caused the ink to swell, then dry, on the paper. As it dried, the paper lifted from the plate, retaining a clear imprint of the design. Any slight imperfections of line in the design could be touched up on the transfer paper with a fine pencil brush. Surplus paper was then trimmed away.

The design had yet to be transferred from this gummed paper to the enamel, but this was a simple process. The paper was moistened with the tongue and laid face down in its required position upon the white enamel surface, a special brush being used to force it flat on to the enamel. After having been left to stand for a time, the enamel, with transfer paper still adhering, was placed in the muffle and subjected to fusing heat, during which the design was burnt into the enamel, or 'made fast', while the paper itself was consumed by the fire and all traces of oil burnt out of the coloured ink. Any colours and shading subsequently applied over this transfer-print naturally required further firing.

The main problem in such transfer-printing was to achieve the right adjustment between the depth of the engraved line and the consistency of the colour so that the print would appear strong yet unblurred. The early Battersea work was sometimes so faint that it required considerable touching-up by hand. But with experience the deeply-cut line engraving of the enamellers was made to produce richly solid and satisfying effects. Such depth of line somewhat limited the scope of the average engraver, however, and for small work, where extremely fine detail was required, another style of transfer-printing was developed. This was known as bat-printing.

The method was introduced into England by William Wynn Ryland in 1760–61 and applied to ceramics about ten years later but to enamels only in about 1780. Its use was confined to small pieces: the minute detail in the picture lids of many little snuff-boxes was achieved in this way.

The process differed considerably from the usual transfer-printing. In the first place, the basis consisted of a stipple engraving, with no more than a

III. *Rose pompadour*, a clear, fresh pink free of the manganese-purple tones, proved a difficult colour for the early enameller, but one which was used with excellent effect when the craft was in its heyday. The box on the left measures $5 \times 3\frac{5}{8} \times 2\frac{1}{2}$ inches, the soft pink ground showing particularly elaborate enrichments. The fine mounts to rim and base are decorated with applied wire ribbon inside and out. The deeper of the two small boxes has the fluted corners associated with many particularly attractive specimens. The third box, in a deeper shade of pink, is decorated on the lid with a stag-hunt scene and on the sides with more simply over-painted transfer-prints. A ring of gilded dots around the base takes the place of a base rim.

subsidiary use of fine line-work, which was well suited to reproducing the delicate detail of a Bartolozzi engraving or a conventional flower posy. Secondly, from the stipple-engraved copper-plate the impression of the design was taken not on transfer paper but on a sheet of pliant material, a quarter of an inch thick, known as a bat. This was made from a preparation of glue, treacle, and whiting, and proved more perfectly receptive than transfer paper. Thirdly, the impression of the design it received when pressed upon the engraved copper-plate was not in colour but in linseed oil. This substance penetrated every detail of the design before the surplus was wiped from the surface of the copper-plate in the usual way, and the flexible bat transferred it with similar exactitude to the enamel. Colour in the form of fine powder dusted over the enamel adhered to the pattern as outlined in the oil. Surplus colour was removed with cotton-wool and the design was fixed by firing in the usual way. Two impressions on enamels were usually obtained from a single application of oil to the bat, which was then washed and used again.

On Battersea work the main transfer-print usually covered the whole surface of box lid or plaque. Gilding appears very seldom on work attributed to Battersea or on early English enamels made elsewhere. But on many of the finest Bilston and Birmingham enamels the final touch of ornament consisted of irregular rococo scrollwork surrounding the painted reserve. This scrolling was in raised enamel, brilliantly gilded.

Early gilders obtained their gold either in leaf form or, less expensively, from gold powder obtained by a chemical precipitation from gold guineas. The gold, ground to a powder, was mixed with oil of lavender to form a paint which was brush-applied to the enamel like any enamel colour, and fired immediately in a muffle. In the nineteenth century gum-water was used instead of the oil of lavender. Early gilding now lacks the brilliance of later work, and even when new it had a slightly dull, though rich, appearance. When applied thickly it could be burnished with a fine agate. Such gilding was not permanent and little has survived.

Not until about 1765 were enamels given more permanent gilded decoration, and even this could not be burnished to attain the rich lustre found on early nineteenth-century porcelain. This gilding was applied to the enamel by a cheaper process, involving the use of mercury and fraught with great danger to the health of the gilder. Gold amalgam was prepared by mixing metallic gold in the form of a fine powder with an equal weight of mercuric oxide and a little alcohol. Later a little bismuth subnitrate might be added. These were well rubbed together and dried at a moderate temperature. The resulting powder was then rubbed with fat oil to produce a soft paste and this was applied to the surface of the enamel with a brush. The mercury was driven off in vapour form by the firing which also fixed the gold. The resulting dull surface required burnishing, and on enamels such gilding may be recognized by its brassy appearance. The process of burnishing consisted in rubbing the gilt surfaces with a smooth bloodstone or agate and cleaning them from time to time with white lead, applied on a piece of sheepskin. Perfect cleanliness was indispensable. The burnisher never handled the enamel except through a piece of clean white linen. The agate was lightly applied, following the lines of the ornaments and never rubbing across them lest the gilding should appear scratched.

Reference has been made to the way in which such gilding was given its opulent relief effect. Although it may sometimes appear to be solid gilding, the body of the raised lines consisted, in fact, of white enamel applied in the desired scrolling patterns, and fired before being painted with a thin layer of the gold mixture.

Chapter Eight

DECORATION: SOURCES AND STYLES

By the methods detailed in the previous chapter a remarkable variety of decoration was achieved on English painted enamels. So durable have they proved that many specimens remain today as distinctive and charming as they were nearly two centuries ago. Some were wholly painted by hand, some were decorated with monochrome transfer-prints, but most were first printed and then brush-decorated so that very little of the prints remained visible. In each class of work there was the widest possible range of quality: no method can be regarded as intrinsically superior. Moreover, in considering the quality of, say, an enamelled box or a tea-caddy, it is necessary to distinguish between the principal decoration on its lid or front and the minor decoration on the sides, and perhaps inside and on the base.

Directly and indirectly, a number of individuals often contributed to the main decoration of what were, at their best, exceedingly delightful and individualistic creations. Only when their various rôles are appreciated is it possible to understand the reasons underlying the great variety of quality sometimes found in a single decorated enamel.

Most remote from the eventual enamel were the painters of the original pictures which usually formed the basis of the more notable decorations on plaques, box lids, and so on. Until an Act was passed in 1842, no artist was safe from the doubtful compliment of having his published work copied and adapted for industrial purposes without either acknowledgement or fee. At this period the most highly decorative pictorial style was largely the province of French artists, and it is scarcely surprising to find the works of Watteau, Lancret, Boucher, and Nattier figuring largely on such pieces. For instance, there are Antoine Watteau's gay scenes: his *Fêtes Champêtres* (Plate 11), his *Le Colin-Maillard*, engraved by Brion (Plate 12), and the frequently represented mandoline-player from *La Cascade*. There are Nicolas Lancret's 'Flute Lesson' (*Le Maître Galant*) and the many extremely free adaptations of his 'Tea Party'. There are *Les Amants*, by Jean-Marc Nattier (Plate 41), and *Pensent-ils au Raisin?*, by François Boucher. Boucher's *La Belle Aventure*, adapted from the engraving by P. Aveline (Plate 59), showing two shepherdesses and an old fortune-teller, was particularly popular and is to be found notably well reproduced, but all these subjects and very many more appear in varying qualities of transfer-print and colour-wash on eighteenth-century English enamels.

For the other main source of picture subjects, however, the enamellers did not have to look so far. Portraits in plenty were produced in England in the second half of the eighteenth century. The Battersea factory specialized in finely engraved prints by Ravenet of George II, his son Frederick Prince of Wales, Frederick's son Prince George, William Augustus, Duke of Cumberland, and so on. But many other portraits on transfer-printed enamels date from long after the closing of York House, being copied from well-known prints whose dates are established. These subjects include Prince William Henry (later William IV) upon entering the Navy in 1779; General Eliott, of Gibraltar fame, 1779; Admiral Rodney, 1780; General Clinton, who captured Charleston in 1780, and many others. The beauties of the day were painted too, and the paintings widely copied in mezzotint engravings. The portraits of the Gunning sisters by Francis Cotes (Plate 2) and of Ann Day, afterwards Lady Fenhoulet (Plate 34), who was painted by Sir Joshua Reynolds, in 1757 and 1760, are obvious examples widely reproduced on enamels. Thomas Gainsborough, Thomas Worlidge, Allan Ramsay, and William Hoare (source of the portrait of William Pitt on Sadler and Green enamels) are other portraitists whose work was copied extensively.

Only slightly less remote was the association between the enamel decoration and the men who produced the mezzotint engravings from these original oil paintings and thus made them generally familiar—and, therefore, in popular demand. Before the era of photography, such expert mezzotint engravers were the usual link between artist and public. A familiar picture as reproduced upon an enamel frequently contains details which indicate clearly enough that the decorator's source has been an imperfect engraving rather than the original painting.

Among these engravers may be mentioned Richard Houston, pupil of John Brooks, who popularized Philippe Mercier's series representing 'Morning', 'Afternoon', and so on: the charmingly vivacious study of a woman holding a mask from 'Night' in this series is one of the paintings, or over-painted transfer-prints, most frequently encountered on well-mounted étuis and dainty scent bottles (Plate 65). Nicolas de Larmessin and J.-P. Le Bas are associated with the engravings of Lancret's work. Richard Purcell and James McArdell engraved some Reynolds portraits, McArdell's work including the engraving of Catherine Chambers, wife of the architect, familiar on enamels. Le Veau and François Vivares produced many engravings of classical landscapes which, like Panini's Italian architecture and various seaport views, appeared on innumerable painted enamels. Vivares's engraving, usually known as 'The Return from the Hunt', is to be found in reproductions that show every quality of workmanship in the transfer engraving and over-painting. Other pastoral scenes were based on the work of such artists as Luke Sullivan, part of whose engraved 'View of Woobourn', chiefly consisting of a milkmaid and cows, is familiar as a black transfer-print which has been ascribed to Robert Hancock.

The enamel decorations that come in the landscape category deserve special mention if only because there are so many of them. In considering their merits, it must be remembered that at this period in England landscape painting was scarcely yet acceptable unless it followed the classical trend of Claude Lorrain. The first great English landscapist, Richard Wilson, found this to his cost; significantly, even in reproduction on enamel, it is as the portraitist he never wished to be that he is recorded—for example, in the picturesque little study of Prince George. These classical landscapes on enamels, as on contemporary European porcelains and costly wall-papers, are pleasantly drawn and carefully coloured, but they are largely unambitious, routine pieces of work, strictly in accordance with the current demand for pillared ruins, groups of cattle and sheep, rivers, and people picturesquely posed against the 'Romantic Rocks form'd by Art to Embellish the Prospect', as illustrated in *The Ladies Amusement*. Only very occasionally do people and animals come to life and take charge of such scenes—as in the case of a box in the collection of Her Majesty Queen Mary where the conventional flute-player among the ruins is confronted by a highly unconventional donkey

133

braying in protest. Only comparatively seldom, too, can a topographical subject on an enamel be identified, such as the view of Orleans House, Twickenham, in the collection of Her Majesty Queen Mary, and that of Strawberry Hill in the collection of the Hon. Mrs Ionides.

The engravings which inspired much of this work were intended specifically for the use of contemporary decorators on porcelain, japanning, and so on. Hancock's engravings of designs by Boitard were referred to in Chapter Three. J. H. O'Neale, C. Fenn, and very many other designers for industrial artists could be mentioned in this connection. The book by 'Pillement and Others', entitled *The Ladies Amusement; or, Whole Art of Japanning Made Easy*, was but one of these pattern books, published in about 1760, its two hundred plates illustrating more than fifteen hundred patterns, which were used extensively in industrial art for more than twenty years. The 1760's and 1770's saw the publication of *The Artist's Vade-mecum, The Draughtsman's Assistant, The Designer's Assistant,* and so on.

Sometimes painters in the enamellers' employ made direct free-hand copies of such designs on to the enamels. Much more often the enamellers commissioned or employed engravers who copied these designs, or parts of them, on to their own copper-plates, often without troubling to work in reverse even when the subject was a portrait. From these plates they then took paper transfers which would print the designs on to a considerable number of enamels. This was the method that Brooks introduced at Battersea. Janssen was exceptionally fortunate in being able to call on the very considerable engraver Simon-François Ravenet to make many of his engravings, including some original work. Other enamellers had often to depend on lesser men for the engraved plates that supplied their transfers. Some of these even made their own engravings of designs originally engraved by Ravenet.

As many engravers to the enamellers and potters of eighteenth-century England worked as freelances supplying more than one factory, similarities of engraving technique are little use in any attempt to attribute enamels to one particular maker. Such an engraver had not necessarily any position inside the enamelling factory. Other technicians took the paper transfers from his engraved copper-plates and applied them to the enamel. Their combination and arrangement was left to the discretion of the enameller.

To instance one small example, there is a box in the Ionides collection (Plate 30) decorated on lid and sides and base with transfer-prints of the music and words of a *gavotte*, an *ariette*, and two *menuets*—at a period when the 'plugging' of popular music was restricted to such dainty trifles as enamels and fans. The lid decoration of this box is similar to that of No. 343 in the Schreiber collection, whereas the sides resemble those of Nos. 158, 343, 355. And inside the lid, each of these boxes is treated entirely differently, that in the Ionides collection bearing a transfer-print portrait delicately coloured.

If the engraver had little voice in the arrangement of his transfer-prints, he probably had equally little control of the subsequent over-painting which gave the majority of the more important enamels their final character. It is very necessary to emphasize this. Apart from the early work particularly associated with Battersea, in which untinted monochrome transfer-printing was prevalent, and which was dominated by Ravenet, the decoration of eighteenth-century English enamels depended in large measure upon the artistic abilities of employee-painters who applied the colours over the faint lines of the underlying transfer-print. Even in monochrome work the transfer-print was generally touched up with over-painting, transparent or opaque. Some colourists used the stippling technique of painters on ivory; some painted details of face and feature with the delicacy of the miniature artist. But the general run of these workers, applying heavy, opaque pigments, entirely concealed the underlying transfer-printed lines. This accounts for many a painting in which fundamentally good draughtsmanship is hastily, sometimes crudely, coloured.

There were, of course, many exceptions. Enamels are found which are so entirely individualistic that they are obviously painted as unique little works of art rather than as commercial propositions. For instance, in the Ionides collection is a fascinating 'family' box (Plate 39). On the lid is depicted a wedding in a church. On the sides are scenes of everyday life—children at play, men reaping, quarrying, and gardening. On the base is shown a funeral procession, and inside the lid are inscribed the names of ten people who died between 1741 and 1763.

Even the simpler painted work generally appears to have undergone at least two firings; much more complex treatment was given to some of the more ornate work, such as the handsome harbour scenes which crowd the lids of some early boxes.

In addition to the principal decoration on the lid, enamel boxes of every kind usually had side and end decorations, frequently by a different painter or from an entirely different set of transfers. It is among these minor decorations, and in the tiny reserves on thimbles and bodkin-holders, the shoulders of tea-caddies, and the bases of candlesticks and the like, that there is most evidence of recourse to the pattern books of the day. The fishing group (Colour Plate II), the man with the dog and gun, Hancock's man and woman walking together (Plate 65), and other similar minor studies from *The Ladies Amusement* are frequently found on the sides of boxes and étuis. Even swags of flowers 'after ye French Taste' are abundantly featured in this book, as well as the ships, cattle, butterflies, insects, flowers, and so on, drawn and engraved by a wide variety of artists, including Pillement, Fenn, J. June, Hemerich, and others besides the more familiar Robert Hancock. The 'Chinese' groups which dominate the book are found comparatively seldom on enamels: the craze found adequate expression in porcelain and japanning. But perhaps the most significant conclusion to be reached from studying such pattern books of the period is the fact that not even such an abundance of models could make eighteenth-century enamellers lose their individuality and become slavish copyists.

A box or a tobacco-press (Plate 72), for example, may be decorated with a delightful assemblage of a dozen birds, of precisely the type engraved by P. Benazech in *The Ladies Amusement* from drawings by C. Fenn, and yet not one of the birds be identical with Fenn's examples. The châtelaine and accompanying étui in the late Queen Mary's collection has no fewer than eleven tiny reserves individually decorated with pastoral scenes, yet no two are alike. The flowers, most prolific of all the enamel decorator's devices, became progressively simpler, losing the ornate Oriental influence of early porcelain work in favour of a meticulous Dutch manner, but to a remarkably large extent those tulips, honeysuckles, and ever-recurrent blue convolvulus flowers conveyed the impression of having been painted from real flowers rather than from commercial copy-books. This quality of individuality was eventually lost: mass production methods dictated a return to plain transfer-printing or, at best, an occasional dab of colour, but such late work is by no means characteristic of English enamel painters of the eighteenth century.

71. The lids of three boxes which suggest the possible existence of an enamel works at Pontypool (see page 85). The boxes are of japanned iron, the lids mounted with painted enamel plaques. The large box lid, measuring $7\frac{1}{2} \times 5\frac{1}{4}$, has a metal mirror on its interior surface, framed in gilt-metal. The undersides of the smaller box lids, $4\frac{5}{8} \times 4$ inches, have enamels painted with flowers and insects.

72. Sometimes regarded as a tea-caddy, this tobacco-box contains an enamelled press with a knob handle, also painted with birds, to fit closely over the contents. The underside of the press and the box have been French plated, now appearing a pewter grey. The whole decoration suggests that its source was *The Ladies Amusement* which contains many bird designs by C. Fenn engraved by P. Benazech. The scrolls of flowers are a Pillement design, engraved by Hemerich from the same book and described as 'After ye French taste'.

73. Among the most magnificent products of the enamellers was the outfit comprising tea-canisters and sugar-box in a locked tea-chest. In this example the ground colour is a soft pink with white diapers and richly gilded scrolls. The chest has convex sides lined and partitioned with velvet-covered wood. Metal mounts protect all the exposed edges, attached with tiny rivets. The hinge extends the full width of the box and matches the handsome scroll-and-flower handles. The tea-canisters and sugar-box are ornamented in keeping with the pastoral scenes on the chest.

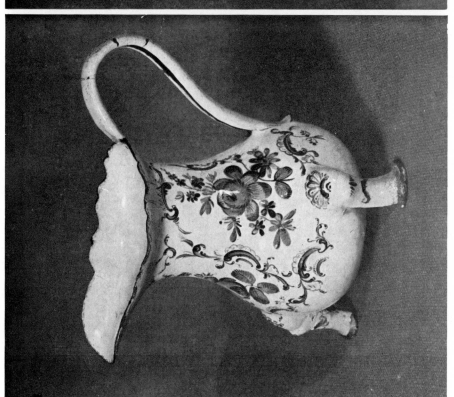

74. An example of enamelled ware dating to late in the eighteenth century, and designed to sell to an ever-widening public. The jug is painted with flowers in full colour surrounded by purple flowering scrolls on a white ground. The handle is channelled, its inner surface not enamelled, and the feet are hollow.

75. A hot-water jug, 10 inches high, which presented constructional problems to the makers of the metal core under the enamel. On the neck and near the base may be seen slight swellings where the shaped pieces of metal were joined together before enamelling. The handle is round and enamel covered and the base is of notably thick enamel to take the rub of wear.

139

76. Elaborate and exceedingly decorative candlesticks were evolved by the South Staffordshire and Birmingham enamellers, tall examples being made in parts until muffle size was increased. The assembly of a varied range of parts allowed of considerable differences between designs. The pair illustrated here are joined by metal rims to their square supports, and the rich note of gilt-metal is emphasized in the screwed-on swags shaped in full relief and the metal bases. The candle nozzles are loose and can be inverted as is seen in the central example, which displays a decorative finial. Ground colour is turquoise blue, with dark blue and yellow decoration and full-colour painting.

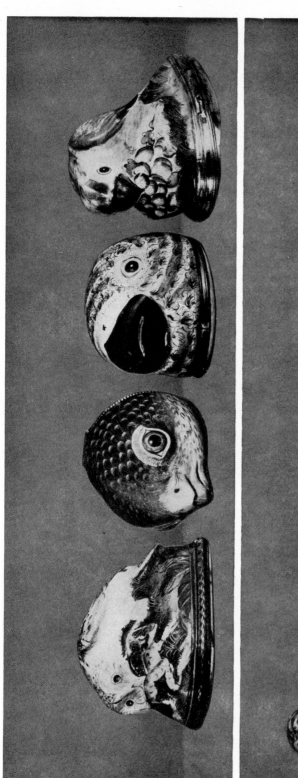
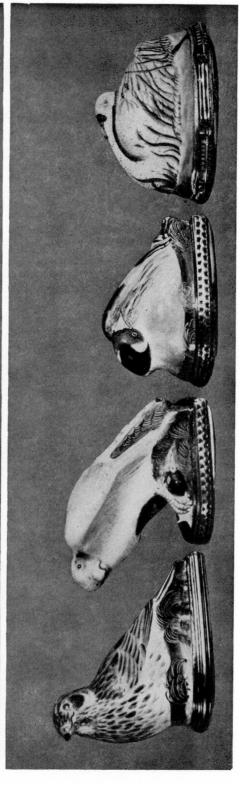

77. Some of the finest of the modelled boxes or bonbonnières are of birds and birds' heads, in the style of Meissen work. These brilliant examples bear detailed examination of their excellent design and meticulous workmanship. The opening is usually in the base, the bird resting on the slightly convex 'lid' which is also decorated. In many examples base and model are directly related, such as the crouching eagle which has a base painted with a cock, hen and chicks disturbed by the bird overhead. This is not invariable, however: the owl with a frog has a base picture of a scolding magpie.

141

78. Standish, 9×6 inches, complete with containers for pounce, taper and shot (to clean the quills) and ink. The tray is constructed from a single piece of metal, the edges bent down to form the base and finished without metal mounts. The river scene on the quill rack was particularly popular with the enamellers and also appeared on the sides of snuff and tobacco boxes.

79. Another type of standish tray, 6×3 inches. Much of the decorative effect is achieved by perforation of the rim which, as it requires no metal mount, can be given a scalloped edge. The piece appears to have been dipped into liquid enamel of a milky white. The square glass bottles have facet-cut shoulders and rough punty marks on their bases. The enamelled lids are flower-decorated.

80. A pair of salts, the ground colour deep purplish-pink with painted and gilt decoration. The dipping method of applying the enamel made possible the introduction of much ornamental perforation, the liquid enamel flowing over the raw edges of the metal core. The salts themselves are riveted to the tray, white enamelled inside, and each painted on the outside with three tiny full-colour pictures, the corresponding picture identical on each salt and on other sets from the same factory.

81. Examples of quickly but effectively decorated work, the metal cores dipped in liquid enamel and hand-decorated on both sides of their serrated rims, as well as on the flat central areas. The bird on the right was a popular subject derived from a Hancock engraving in *The Ladies Amusement*.

82. A set of trays with perforated rims, the large one $5\frac{1}{8} \times 4\frac{1}{2} \times 1\frac{1}{4}$ inches, the small one $3\frac{1}{2} \times 3\frac{1}{8} \times 1\frac{1}{4}$ inches. The metal core of each tray has been rolled over at the rim before enamelling to give the piece an appearance of greater thickness. The rims are white inside, purplish-pink outside with a little floral decoration and edgings of blue and gilt.

143

Cloakpins with enamel Pictures set in stampt Metal rims burnished of a fine Gold Colour

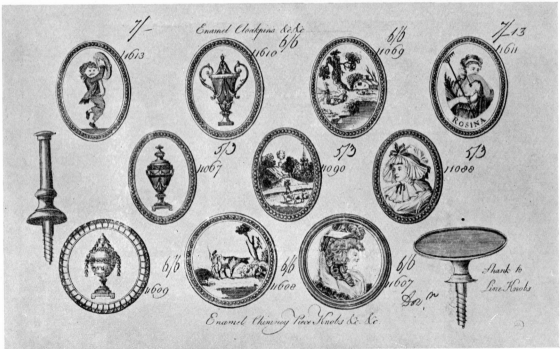

Enamel Chimney Piece Knobs &c &c

83. Two pages from a pattern book illustrating minor uses for enamels, transfer-printed and often quickly washed with colour. The book is undated, its publisher unknown, but appears to have been issued about 1780. These designs were intended for cloakpins and chimney-piece knobs. Many sets of buttons were made, too, the tiny enamels similarly mounted in frames of machine-stamped gilt-metal.

Chapter Nine

MOUNTS

THE final stage in the production of a decorated enamel was the attachment of a metal frame or mount. This was necessitated by the nature of the enamelling methods used until nearly the end of the eighteenth century. The base enamel, applied with a spatula to both faces of the thin sheet of copper, could not be made to adhere firmly to the sharp edges of the metal: if these were exposed to use there was always the risk of flaking. The Georgian enamellers met this problem by binding all exposed edges in thin frames of copper or copper alloy.

Plaques were simply framed, generally with narrow bands of lightly punched or tooled metal, but considerable importance was attached to the mounts of many other enamelled trinkets. Every type of box had a double rim of metal at the edges where box and lid met; usually the whole of one long side was occupied by the hinge. But many good quality boxes also had metal rimming their bases to protect the enamel on the sharp angle between side and base, and some caskets had ribbons of metal on the vertical angles of the sides (Plate 53). A delicate étui would have rims of metal at top and base as well as along the edges where lid and body met, and even the tiniest scent bottle had a metal lip rim in addition to the decorated metal stopper attached by a slender chain (Plate 64).

In the announcement of the sale at York House, Battersea, there is a reference to 'copper frames for mounting the enamels', and it has generally been assumed that the Battersea enamels were all mounted in copper, in contrast to the brighter, brassier products of South Staffordshire. In the list of enamels to be sold from Janssen's own home, however, which presumably were outstanding examples kept there as specimens, the description reads 'mostly mounted in metal, double-gilt'. This suggests the use of mounts made of a copper alloy.

Copper was necessary as the base on to which the enamels were fired, but it was regarded as an expensive material. Most of that used in the enamelling industry was supplied by the Ecton Hill Copper Mine, in Staffordshire, where, in 1769, no fewer then three hundred men, women, and children were employed, working a seventy-two-hour week. The men—and in those days these included boys over eleven years old—could reach a top wage of twopence an hour; women, employed as ore-breakers, fourpence to eightpence a day; boys and girls, on haulage and sorting jobs, threepence and twopence a day.

Copper alloys were developed mainly, of course, with a view to serving as cheap substitutes for gold. One of the best known was pinchbeck, which had such a considerable resemblance to gold that in 1734 Fielding wrote of an unfortunate goldsmith 'the nobility and gentry run so much into Pinchbeck that he had not disposed of two gold watches this month'.

This alloy, developed by the Fleet Street watch and clock maker, Christopher Pinchbeck, consisted of about five parts of copper to one part of zinc; but other, cheaper proportions of the constituents were often used, tending more nearly to the consistency of brass (two parts of copper to one part of zinc). As these alloys were applied to the mounts of enamels much of the coppery undertone associated with early work disappeared. One of the most popular copper-zinc alloys for these mounts was bath metal, in which almost half the weight of metal consisted of the cheaper zinc; in very similar platina even less copper was introduced. These alloys were excellent for their purpose. Being very ductile, they were easily rolled into thin plates from which strips could be cut and hand-shaped to fit the enamels. At the time of their manufacture their basic colour and their tendency to tarnish were of no consequence as they were generally given a double-gilt finish by a dangerous and laborious process involving the use of mercurial chemicals.

Such alloys were still imperfect, however, and mount-makers found that they required frequent annealing if they were to be kept soft and pliable while being shaped. Not until 1781 did James Emerson of Bristol patent an invention for the direct alloying of zinc to copper which was the basis of modern brass-founding. Watson, reporting on the Emerson alloy in his

Chemical Essays, published shortly after its introduction to the brass industry, wrote that the metal was 'more beautiful, more malleable, and of a colour more resembling gold than any other brass'. There was an immediate demand for this new metal among the toy makers of Birmingham. Mount-makers everywhere found it excellent for producing work which was intrinsically cheaper and, because it did not readily oxidize, seldom required the added expense of gilding.

Birmingham, Bilston, and Wolverhampton were the principal suppliers of mounts to the enamel trade, although some mounts came from London. Benjamin Cartwright, Strand, London, is reputed to have made mounts for Battersea. Anyone with a liking for neat metalcraft can appreciate the superb standard of much of this eighteenth-century work. Sufficient indication of quality is the fact that innumerable little enamel boxes survive in perfect working order after nearly two centuries of endless opening and closing. Yet the metal rims were applied without adhesive, and so perfect was the fit between lid and body that no form of hasp or spring was ever considered necessary, even when the box was designed for powder or snuff.

Throughout the period under review these mounts were constructed by hand from flat metal ribbon, but the methods by which this ribbon was shaped and decorated were rapidly developed. Undoubtedly the Birmingham firm of Boulton and Fothergill served this country well in establishing standards of workmanship appreciated on the Continent as well as in this country.

In the earliest mounts the metal ribbon was comparatively plain, for even the simplest shaping or decoration had to be hand-applied. The metal was merely cast in bricks which were rolled out into thin sheets, and these sheets were cut up into short, narrow strips which could be rolled individually to the thinness finally required. Decoration on mounts made from these strips was obviously restricted to such flat, tooled lines and punchings as the mount-maker's time and ingenuity allowed.

The first improvement in technique came in 1768. This was the introduction of a steel swage-block through which the ribbon of softer metal could be drawn so that its cross-section or profile was of any ornamental shape that might be wanted. The sides of the two-piece block were shaped as required and the metal necessarily assumed similar contours as it was pulled between them.

These swage-shaped ribbons were too flimsy to be used alone as mounts. Instead, they were hard-soldered to slightly heavier, plain ribbons which were formed into the mounts. Such built-up mounts are distinctive and are associated with enamels made before the era of cut-price mass-production. Surface and edge decoration on this moulded ribbon was still hand-applied, however, such simple motifs as gadrooning and beading being punched upon it. The inevitable irregularities of handwork distinguish them from machine-made patterns. The latter date from 1779 onwards, for in that year William Bell patented a method of decorating the outer surface of profiled ribbons by means of 'rolling cylinders, the cylinders being shaped to suit the design. These are of great benefit to the toy trade.'

By then mount-making had become a highly specialized craft which might be divided into more than fifty operations, although the actual construction of each mount remained a hand operation, requiring considerable skill. Specialization did not begin in the toy trade until about 1770, but was complete within ten years. By then the use of the stamp and the press had created new trades, and outworkers were employed on many of the processes. At first even plaque frames were produced by mount-makers, but from about 1775 the majority came from specialist metal frame-makers.

Mounts for boxes, caddies, étuis, and so on with close-fitting lids joined with hinges were known in the enamel trade as 'jointed mounts'. Most of the hinges were particularly well made, but showed a slight deterioration of workmanship from about 1795. Hinges on the inexpensive souvenir boxes were never of such high quality as those found on finely painted enamels. Sometimes these cheap hinges had only three joints; the usual number was five, as contrasted with the many found in the hinges that extended the full width of the backs of large caskets (Plate 73). On reproduction enamels the marks of the press tools are often clearly visible around the hinges, and in many instances the hinge shows a small central projection.

Even on boxes with extremely well-made jointed mounts the use of metal base-strips was limited. In general, these appeared only on boxes with straight sides making square, sharp angles with their bases. Many other boxes had slightly concave sides, the curves continuing in S-outline to round smoothly into the flat area of the base (Plate 12). The sharp angle liable to chip and flake was thus avoided. In some cases the colour washed over the sides of the box was continued over the base; in others the line where coloured sides met white base was decorated with a row of raised gilded dots in lieu of a metal base rim.

It has been stressed that the raw edges of the enamel were of necessity covered with metal mounts. This rule held good as long as the coatings of enamel were applied to the copper with a spatula. The process of dipping, described in Chapter Six, offered new possibilities to the price-cutting enameller, however. On these dipped pieces the extremely fluid enamel 'took' in a thin film even on the edges of the copper: hence the development of various pierced decorations never previously attempted.

The most exposed edges of the little counter trays (Plate 82), standishes (Plate 79), and so on, made on this principle, required more careful treatment, however. Usually a slightly rounded surface, to which the enamel would adhere more strongly, was provided by folding back the very edge of the underlying copper. The enamel into which it was dipped entirely filled the crevice formed at the edge of the fold and the piece was merely given the appearance of being of slightly thicker material than was in fact the case. A jug handle, subjected to particularly hard wear, might consist of a fully rounded tube, completely enamelled (Plate 75), or of a strip of metal, its edges turned in roundly and not flatly, enamelled only on the outer surface (Plate 74). Such an avoidance of mounts, however, while broadening the scope of the enameller's work, was symptomatic of the craft's decline. It is impossible to imagine Stephen Theodore Janssen or Matthew Boulton tolerating such productions.

Very many mount-makers in Bilston served the painted enamel trade. Among others may be mentioned: Samuel Howard, 1770–93; John Ellidge, 1770–85 (?); William Bibbins, 1765–84; Samuel Stone, whose stock was sold in 1758; John Pilson, 1768–82; Thomas Perry, 1780–95 (?); the Moss family, including Edward, William, and Joseph, 1770–91. A descendant of this family told the authors that his family made mounts for the Beckett firm and in direct consequence became prosperous, only to lose their fortune again when large quantities of goods which they supplied to another firm went unpaid for, having been shipped to France immediately before the Revolution.

Wolverhampton mount-makers known by the authors, through personal contact with their descendants, to have supplied Bilston and Wednesbury enamellers, include: Richard Shinton, 1770–90 (?); John and Henry Brett, 1770–80; William Spink, 1780–90. The Spink family, with workshops in Stafford Street, Wolverhampton, supplied the Yardley firm at Wednesbury with inexpensive mounts almost to the end. A box containing about one hundredweight of faulty mounts was sold as scrap in about 1911.

Among the Birmingham mount-makers supplying enamellers were: John

Pickering, 1761–80 (?); William Phillips, 1770–80; Lee and Gimblett, 1768–(?); Thomas Wilmore, 1770–93; John Marston, 1765–90.

It must be obvious to the reader that such lists are still far from complete. Others will doubtless take up the tale where this book leaves it and will find answers to many of the problems here presented. That, surely, must be one of the main purposes of such a monograph. Only by a slow and cautious accumulation of facts, and an equally honest rejection of earlier and unsubstantiated theories, can the sum of real knowledge be increased, and a wider understanding thus bring its own satisfaction in a deeper enjoyment of trifles whose very essence was to delight.

INDEX